Interdisziplinäre Verortungen
der Angewandten Linguistik

Band 18

Herausgegeben von
Sylwia Adamczak-Krysztofowicz, Silvia Bonacchi,
Przemysław Gębal, Jarosław Krajka, Łukasz Kumięga
und Hadrian Lankiewicz

Die Bände dieser Reihe sind peer-reviewed.

Przemysław E. Gębal / Karol Krzyżosiak (eds.)

Polish as a foreign and second language among Ukrainian migrants

With 6 figures

V&R unipress

POLISH NATIONAL AGENCY
FOR ACADEMIC EXCHANGE

MIX
Papier aus verantwor-
tungsvollen Quellen
FSC® C083411

Bibliografische Information der Deutschen Nationalbibliothek
Die Deutsche Nationalbibliothek verzeichnet diese Publikation in der Deutschen
Nationalbibliografie; detaillierte bibliografische Daten sind im Internet über
https://dnb.de abrufbar.

Diese Publikation wurde finanziert von der Polnischen Nationalagentur für Akademischen
Austausch (NAWA) im Rahmen des Projektes „Mapping new agents and trends in teaching Polish
as a foreign language among Ukrainian migrants in Poland" (Grant interwencyjny NAWA
BPN/GIN/2022/1/00088).

Gutachter: Władysław T. Miodunka † (Jagiellonnen-Universität Kraków)

Druck und Bindung: CPI books GmbH, Birkstraße 10, D-25917 Leck
Printed in the EU.

Vandenhoeck & Ruprecht Verlage | www.vandenhoeck-ruprecht-verlage.com

ISSN 2749-0211
ISBN 978-3-8471-1773-5

Contents

**Part Three. New Developments: Woman perspective – Everyday
practice – Netnolinguistics**

In Loving Tribute:
Remembering the Legacy of Prof. Władysław T. Miodunka (1945–2024)

With great sorrow and disbelief, we received the news of the passing of Władysław Miodunka – a remarkable man, an outstanding scientist, and a mentor to many generations of Polish and international scholars in the fields of linguistics, applied linguistics, and glottodidactics. Professor Władysław Miodunka passed away on April 24, 2024. His review of our volume marked his final scientific contribution.

> *The problems of teaching Polish should be placed among the problems of teaching other foreign languages, considering both what they have in common and what divides them. We should also draw attention to the European specificity of these problems.*
> (Miodunka 1977)

Professor Władysław Miodunka was the creator of the theoretical foundations of applied linguistics for teaching Polish as a foreign language and Polish glottodidactics. His academic activity contributed to the creation of an original framework for this area of research, called the Krakow School of Polish Glottodidactics. The concepts developed in Krakow in the field of learning and teaching Polish as a foreign, second and inherited language gained a significant influence and reached the mainstream of global and European trends. According to Professor Miodunka's conception, the academic space of Polish language glottodidactics adopted a Western European orientation from the very beginning, which significantly distinguished it from the concepts of teaching other Slavic languages, for the development of which the didactics of the Russian language was a key point of reference. The development and popularity of the Krakow School was the result of its methodological format of practicing glottodidactic comparativism in relation to the concept developed in the didactics of Western European languages and the European standards of language education created on their basis.

Professor Miodunka learned applied linguistics and European glottodidactics from the best. In the 1970s, he studied linguistics at the University of Le Mirail in Toulouse, France, obtaining the *Diplôme d'Ètudes Approfondies* in 1977. His mental guide to the contemporary concepts of teaching French as a foreign language was Professor Paul Rivenc (1925–2019), co-creator of the assumptions of the audiovisual method for language teaching (*méthodologie structuro-globale audiovisuelle – SGAV*).

Professor Miodunka's broad scientific interests included not only applied linguistics and Polish language glottodidactics. He was also fascinated by ethnic studies, bilingualism and Latin American studies, to which he devoted numerous monographs and collective studies. He was also the author of curricula for teaching Polish as a foreign language and textbooks for learning it. He published, among others, the first ever communicative textbook for teaching Polish as a foreign language for beginners entitled *Cześć, jak się masz?* and the first professional television course *Uczmy się polskiego!*

Extensive publishing activity was undertaken by Professor Miodunka already with the establishment of the Department of Linguistics Applied to Teaching Polish as a Foreign Language in 1980. Known to researchers, as well as lectors and teachers of Polish as a foreign language, the so-called "green series", published in the years 1980–1996, consisted of 46 volumes which were the author's concepts of solving various pedagogical, didactic and methodological problems arising in teaching Polish to foreigners. Its continuation was the series "Polish Language for Foreigners", published by the Krakow scientific publishing house Universitas, in which 34 volumes were published in the years 1996–2011. They included, among others, textbooks popular in Poland and around the world addressed to recipients at various levels of advancement. The Universitas publishing house also published the series "Methodology of Teaching Polish as a Foreign Language" in the years 2004–2011, in which 11 volumes were published. Currently, it is published by the Księgarnia Akademicka publishing house as "Biblioteka LingVariów". Professor Miodunka also published abroad. An important volume for him was the monograph *Didactics of Polish as Foreign and Second Language against the European Background*, published in 2023 as part of the InterVAL series by Vandenhoeck & Ruprecht Verlage (V&R unipress), prepared in cooperation with Prof. Przemysław Gębal, initiator and scientific editor of the series. This volume was a summary of the entire European path of development of Polish language glottodidactics to date. As fate decreed, it also summarized the entire academic activity of Professor Władysław Miodunka.

Didactic work was also an important part of Miodunka's activity, who enjoyed teaching others. In his case, it meant teaching foreigners both at his alma mater and at foreign universities: at Le Mirail University in Toulouse/France (1973–1977), Wayne State University in Detroit/USA (1979–1980), Department of Education in Canberra/Australia (1986), Stanford University in California/USA (1988–1990), Federal University of the State of Parana in Curitiba/Brazil (1995–1996), Lomonosov University in Moscow/Russia (1998). Even after professorship, Władysław Miodunka often continued to conduct practical classes of Polish in Krakow and abroad.

Under the Professor's scientific supervision, numerous doctoral and habilitation theses were written, which established the strong academic position of Polish language glottodidactics. Professor Miodunka was a beloved promoter and mentor who was sincerely happy with the success of his students. "I am here to help you realize your scientific dreams", "You are doomed to success!", "Tell me what you really think on this matter" are examples of expressions that his students would hear from him.

Professor Miodunka promoted many doctors. Over the last 17 years, thanks to his substantive and mentoring support, 9 habilitation theses were written by his students. The following people received their habilitation degrees: Wiesław Stefańczyk (2007), Piotr Horbatowski (2009), Przemysław W Turek (2010), Robert Dębski (2010), Anna Seretny (2011), Iwona Janowska (2012), Ewa Lipińska (2013), Przemysław Gębal (2014) and Waldemar Martyniuk (2014). Professor Przemysław Gębal obtained the title of professor of humanities in 2021.

Thanks to the efforts of Professor Miodunka, in 1980 the Department of Applied Linguistics for Teaching Polish as a Foreign Language was established within the structures of the Jagiellonian University – the first scientific unit in Poland dealing with research on the processes of Polish language education. In 2005, it gained the status of the Department of Polish as a Foreign Language, and in 2017, on its basis, the Institute of Polish Glottodidactics, the only one in Poland and in the world, was established, institutionally crowning the functioning of the Krakow School of Polish Glottodidactics of Prof. Władysław Miodunka.

Every scientific school is a historical phenomenon – emerging, developing and finally disappearing. Its useful life depends on the consistency in implementing the adopted research method and the degree of involvement of specialists forming the school in its scientific continuation.

Professor Miodunka was able to inspire others with his passion and joy. He taught to enjoy life and the development of Polish language glottodidactics, which he had special affection for and treated as his life mission.

We will remember him as an Outstanding Professor who "gave wings to everyone", who told us that we were destined for success. He will remain in our memory as a great and strong man, and at the same time sensitive and open towards others. Publisher of publications, Reviewer, Manager and Scientific Mentor, Vice-Dean of International Studies at the Jagiellonian University (2001–2002) and Vice-Rector of the Jagiellonian University in Krakow (2002–2008).

Goodbye, friend! Your mission will continue, as well as the mission of the Krakow School of Polish Glottodidactics.

Editors

Przemysław E. Gębal / Karol Krzyżosiak (University of Gdańsk)

Polish as a foreign and second language among Ukrainian migrants. An introduction

This book represents an endeavor on the part of applied linguistics to elaborate interdisciplinary knowledge and solutions in response to the unprecedented migration situation in Poland. The migratory processes currently observed are dynamically reshaping the landscape of learning and teaching Polish as a foreign and second language. In recent years, a historical change has been observed in the status of Polish itself: from a local language considered as a tool of adaptation for economic migrants and a relatively rare target of foreign learners and scholars, towards a language that now constitutes a matter of life and death for those fleeing war and repression. While over the last two decades, Polish has gained prestige, facilitating social adaptation and mobility, during times of war, it becomes essential for securing basic living standards, settlement opportunities, and employment prospects. In such circumstances, extracurricular forms of learning become the most common practices at play, as the Polish educational system has never developed a cohesive program of tuition of Polish as a foreign language (PFL) in the context of migration and refugee experience. Furthermore, given the scale of migration, the number and the diversity of newcomers, Polish schools and universities have no capacity to provide tuition for all the people in need. This leads to a spontaneous and chaotic educational situation in which the initiative of teaching Polish is being undertaken by a diverse range of agents, such as refugee centers, non-governmental organizations, private companies and individuals who often lack professional linguistic or didactic background, but wish to share their migrant knowledge and language competence with their compatriots through teaching platforms or social media. Ultimately, the pivotal role of self-education appears as self-evident. Migrants and refugees from Ukraine learn Polish primarily through everyday practice, in workplace and during social interaction, as most of them have no access to any form of systematic tuition. Faced with urgent needs for adaptation and acculturation, individuals with migrant and refugee experiences themselves take charge of enhancing their language skills. Drawing from their learning biographies (Thoma 2022), migrant knowledge (Rajaram 2022), personal beliefs (White 2008) and subjective theories

(Michońska-Stadnik 2013) about language acquisition, they employ intuitive strategies that they themselves consider efficient. They also benefit from inter-comprehension – a phenomenon that favors to some extent mutual under-standing among users of closely related languages. By immersing themselves in Polish cultural contexts, utilizing social media, exploring written and spoken resources, and receiving support from compatriots, as well as Polish friends and colleagues, new learners manage to surmount the language barrier. Their re-markable success in this regard is underscored by preliminary research (Krzy-żosiak 2024, in: Gębal & Janowska 2024).

Given all the considerations presented above, obtaining the foundational knowledge necessary for conducting effective pedagogical and didactic en-deavors becomes primarily an epistemological challenge. Acknowledging the intricate connections between migration and education holds significant im-plications for both research and practical applications in this field (Pamuła-Behrens M., Hennel-Brzozowska 2019). This, in turn, prompts researchers to undertake studies of the phenomena of Polish language learning, teaching and acquisition in context of migration and refugee experience from new per-spectives. The multi-dimensional character of the problem, rooted in societal, educational, psycholinguistic and anthropological contexts, calls for eclectic approaches that include concepts and research methods from multiple domains. Fortunately, linguists are not alone in this endeavor. The research based on psycholinguistic and didactic methods is complemented by conceptual frame-works and methodologies developed by cultural anthropology and migration studies, which is in line with the spirit of modern approaches, such as linguistic anthropology (Ahearn 2017). Thus, the concept of transdisciplinarity (Kita 2012) emerges as the most suitable methodological approach to encompass the inter-play of anthropological, societal, educational, and psycholinguistic factors within the context of Polish as a foreign and second language amidst the migration crisis.

One of the early responses to the problems described above was a research project undertaken by a group of Polish researchers led by prof. Przemysław Gębal, titled *Mapping of new agents and tendencies in tuition of Polish as a foreign language among Ukrainian immigrants in Poland*. The mapping con-cerned two parallel phenomena: on the one hand, new forms of out-of-school teaching, and on the other hand, out-of-school forms and strategies of self-education as part of learning Polish as a foreign or second language. These two intertwining spheres were the subject of research of the project, the main goal of which was to recognize (map) and analyze the discussed phenomena. The pre-liminary results of this initiative were published in the monograph entitled *Theory and Practice of Polish Language Teaching* (Gębal & Janowska 2024), and some further developments of this research are included in the present monograph, along with other contributions that complement the perspective on the current landscape of PFL among Ukrainians.

This volume compiles the most recent studies on Polish language learning, teaching, and acquisition within the context of migration following the Russian invasion of Ukraine in 2022. These studies focus on developing methods, mapping and analyzing various agents involved in the process in both formal and informal, physical and virtual spaces. The presented contributions are organized into three main categories: *Systemic background and methodological challenges, Migrant tuition and intercomprehension*, and *New developments*.

In the first part, the reader is presented with a comprehensive overview of the historical and political conditions that influence the processes of Polish as a Foreign Language (PFL) instruction among migrants in Poland, as examined by social anthropologist Zbigniew Szmyt from Adam Mickiewicz University. This text underscores the scale of demand for PFL tuition among migrants in the face of historical shift in the status of Polish language on the international level. The next study, by Yuliia Vaseiko and Natalia Tsolyk from University of Lutsk, Ukraine, constitutes a review of current state of systemic PFL tuition in Ukraine. It is the first synthesis of this type since the Russian invasion of Ukraine. The third text in this section, by Karol Krzyżosiak of Gdańsk University, presents the first attempt at developing a transdisciplinary methodological model of research in response to the challenges discussed in previous texts. The author establishes the main theoretical concepts of the research, as well as the methods of data collection and analysis.

The second part of this volume focuses on the role of intercomprehension in tuition of Ukrainian migrants and refugees. Opening this section, Jacopo Saturno from the University of Bergamo, Italy, discusses the thesis that intercomprehension can significantly benefit the acquisition of Polish for both L1 speakers of Slavic languages and speakers of other Slavic languages (L2). Following are two complementary empirical studies from Aneta Lewińska and Lucyna Warda-Radys of UG. Both authors present the results of research led among Ukrainian learners with migrant experience from the perspective of Polish teacher. Implicitly, these contributions highlight the significant role of a teacher-researcher in recognizing challenges and developing strategies of systemic PFL tuition for immigrants.

The third part collects studies from research spaces previously unexplored in the context central to this volume. Dominika Izdebska-Długosz from Jagiellonian University of Krakow attempts to establish the determinants of women's acquisition of the Polish language within two years from the outbreak of the war. The topic of women is particularly significant due to their traditional role in Ukrainian households and their ability to maintain contact with the target community through everyday practices. It can be argued, as observed by

Władysław Miodunka in the review of this volume, that the integration of the entire Ukrainian family in Poland largely depends on women's language skills. This shift of focus orienting the research on language adaptation outside of classes, towards everyday experience, finds complementation in the following contribution by Irena Chawrilska, Elżbieta Czapka and Weronika Kamińska-Skrzyńska of UG. The authoresses present a new methodological model adapting communicational microanalysis to conversations between Ukrainian parents and Polish teachers. With Zbigniew Szmyt's next contribution, the learning environment is analyzed from a novel perspective: the researcher becomes a learner. The ethnographer focuses on practices and strategies of language adaptation in a vocational school for migrants that offers immersive, practice-oriented PFL tuition. Finally, in Karol Krzyżosiak's following contribution, the research enters the virtual sphere, where the author analyzes forms of PFL tuition among Ukrainian teachers and learners on TikTok. In this text, the author employs the novel approach of *netnolinguistics* developed to explore the learning strategies and communicational patterns in digital space of social media.

Closing the volume is a synthetic contribution by Przemysław E. Gębal of UG, proposing the application of the concepts of differentiation and personalization in relation to teaching Polish to Eastern Slavs (Russians, Belarusians and Ukrainians). The article discusses emerging trends in the implementation and organization of Polish language education within the migration context. It explores future directions for developing teaching concepts within evolving social, educational, and professional landscapes.

Summary

Human development in the context of migration is an issue entangled in a number of psychological, social, cultural and linguistic factors that determine the progressive process of acculturation in a new living environment. It is also determined by the openness of the host community, on which the success of all activities aimed at the integration and inclusion of arriving foreigners depends (Gębal 2018, Gębal & Miodunka 2023).

The above-mentioned aspects of Polish learning and tuition among Ukrainians are of significant interest in contemporary education, particularly within the context of migration. One of its essential elements is language education, which, on the one hand, aims to develop immigrants' language skills, and on the other hand, should support the above-mentioned integration and inclusion goals in the cultural and social dimensions (Gębal & Janowska 2024).

The outbreak of the war in Ukraine significantly strengthened the need for a systemic organization of Polish education in the context of migration. It created a number of new educational needs and new, previously unknown strategies for acquiring and learning Polish as a non-native language. In the Polish linguistic educational arena, in addition to institutionalized forms of linguistic and cultural education, a number of new independent, informal and semi-formal educational entities (agents) have appeared, which, considering the diversity of the educational environment, propose new types of didactic and integration activities. They also determine the development of academic Polish language glottodidactics, setting new cognitive goals and innovative paths for further development.

References

Ahearn Laura N. (2017) Living Language – An Introduction to Linguistic Anthropology. Wiley Blackwell, Oxford.

Gębal P.E. (2018) Podstawy dydaktyki języka polskiego jako drugiego. Podejście integracyjno-inkluzyjne. Kraków: Księgarnia Akademicka.

Gębal P.E., Janowska I. (eds.) (2024) Theory and Practice of Polish Language Teaching. New Methodological Concepts. Göttingen: Vandenhoeck & Ruprecht Verlage (V&R unipress).

Heeringa, Wilbert & Gooskens, Charlotte & Van Heuven, Vincent J. (2023) Comparing Germanic, Romance and Slavic: Relationships among linguistic distances. Lingua 287. 103512. (doi:10.1016/j.lingua.2023.103512)

Hentschel, Gerd & Taranenko, Oleksandr & Zaprudski, Siarhej. (2014) Trasjanka und Suržyk – gemischte weißrussisch-russische und ukrainisch-russische Rede. Peter Lang. (doi:10.3726/978-3-653-05057-8)

Hufeisen, Britta & Marx, Nicole (eds.) (2007) EuroComGerm – die sieben Siebe: germanische Sprachen lesen lernen (Reihe EuroComGerm). Aachen: Shaker.

Jarosz S., Klaus W. (eds.) (2023) Polska szkoła pomagania. Przyjęcie osób uchodźczych z Ukrainy w Polsce w 2022 roku. Warszawa: Konsorcjum Migracyjne.

Kita, M. (2012) Razem: konsiliencja, interdyscyplinarność, transdyscyplinarność. In: M. Kita, M. Ślawska (eds.) "Transdyscyplinarność badań nad komunikacją medialną. T. 1, Stan wiedzy i postulaty badawcze" (pp. 11–30). Wydawnictwo Uniwersytetu Śląskiego, Katowice.

Michońska-Stadnik A. (2013) Teoretyczne i praktyczne podstawy weryfikacji wybranych teorii subiektywnych w kształceniu nauczycieli języków obcych. Wydawnictwo Uniwersytetu Wrocławskiego, Wrocław.

Paltridge B. (2020) "Multi-perspective research" in: J. McKinley, H. Rose (eds.) The Routledge Handbook of Research Methods in Applied Linguistics. Routledge, New York.

Pamuła-Behrens M., Hennel-Brzozowska A. (eds.) (2019) Migration and Education. To Understand Relations between Migration and Education – Challenges for Research and Practice. Oficyna Wydawnicza Impuls, Kraków.

Rajaram Prem Kumar (2022) Refugee and migrant knowledge as historical narratives. Routledge, University of Helsinki. DOI: 10.4324/9781003092421-4 Refugees and Knowledge Production.

Saturno, Jacopo (2022) Production of inflectional morphology in intercomprehension-based language teaching: the case of Slavic languages. International Journal of Multilingualism 19(3). 383–401. (doi:10.1080/14790718.2020.1730379)

Schöne K., Gębal P.E., Kołsut S. (2015) Berufsspezifische Sprachkompetenzprofile. Dresden: Technische Universität.

Thoma N. (2022) Biographical perspectives on language ideologies in teacher education. Language and Education, Volume 36, issue 5.

White C. (2008) Beliefs and good language learners. Cambridge University Press, Cambridge.

Part One.
Systemic background and methodological challenges

Zbigniew Szmyt (Adam Mickiewicz University in Poznań)

Polish among Ukrainians. The perspective of migration studies

Abstract

This paper explores teaching Polish as a foreign language amidst migration, shaped by historical shifts, such as Poland's EU accession and Russian-Ukrainian conflicts. Over 25 years, Poland's mono-ethnic society transformed into a multicultural one, fueled by migration from diverse countries, mainly Ukraine and Belarus. This led to increased demand for Polish language education for social integration. The study examines challenges and grassroots initiatives for migrant language education, highlighting its importance for social cohesion and inclusive policies.

Migrations and the language issue

Teaching major world languages such as English, German, French, Portuguese, Russian, Spanish, or Chinese is supported by a comprehensive infrastructure that includes language-promoting institutes worldwide (e. g., the Confucius Institute, the British Council, Alliance Française), professional instructors, textbooks, multimedia materials, dictionaries, and online teaching platforms. The popularity of most of these languages, especially the European ones, can be explained historically through colonial expansion, as well as contemporary economic dominance by countries such as the USA, China, and the UK in the global market. Setting aside discussions of linguistic imperialism (Phillipson 1992), it can be said that proficiency in these languages is a source of social prestige and an important professional skill. Teaching major world languages has itself become a huge business. The situation is different for regional and national languages, whose proficiency is not useful outside the country where the language is used, and the overwhelming majority of its users are native speakers of the respective ethnic group. This was essentially the situation with the Polish language in the post-World War II period.

Unlike socialist times, in recent decades Poland has become a destination for mass migration and refuge, and Polish society has become multicultural.

Therefore, it is necessary to shed light on the migratory context of teaching Polish as a foreign language. The nature, dynamics of migration, age and gender structure of migrants, as well as migration scenarios, the relationship between migrants and the host society, legalization procedures – all these factors ultimately shape new trends in teaching the Polish language. The following paper presents the main migratory trends in post-socialist Poland in the context of teaching the Polish language.

One state, one nation, one language

The Polish People's Republic was almost mono-ethnic and normatively mono-linguistic. Paradoxically, the main demand of nationalist ideology, according to which linguistic and ethnic boundaries should align (Gellner 1983: 5), was only realized in selected communist states such as Poland and the Democratic People's Republic of Korea. Contrary to appearances, mono-ethnicity and mono-lingualism within one state were not a political reflection of "natural" social processes, but resulted from Joseph Stalin's authoritarian decisions and his nationality policy.

Post-war Poland experienced a shift of borders from east to west. In this way, Polish borderlands (Eastern Frontier) were incorporated into Soviet republics: Lithuania, Belarus, and Ukraine. On the other hand, a significant part of East Prussia was incorporated into Poland. Border shifts were accompanied by deportations of populations. Ethnic Poles displaced from the territories annexed by the Soviet Union were sent to Poland, while the majority of Ukrainians and Belarusians were sent from Socialist Poland to the USSR. At the same time, a massive expulsion of the German population from the so-called Recovered Territories took place, i.e., from the territories annexed by Poland at the expense of Germany. The unification of Poland was completed by Operation Vistula – the codename for the 1947 forced resettlement of close to 150,000 Ukrainians and Carpatho-Rusyns from the south-eastern provinces to the Recovered Territories (Motyka 2023: 281–195). Ukrainian-speaking deported families were settled dispersedly and were prohibited from publicly speaking their native language for faster assimilation.

Another action of ethnic and linguistic cleansing in communist Poland was the expulsion to Israel of 13,000 Holocaust survivors of Polish Jews as part of the Anti-Zionist Campaign in 1968 (Stola 2007: 298). Linguistic and ethnic minorities from Silesia and Pomerania were either forcibly Polonized or stigmatized as representatives of neighboring nations and pushed out of the country. This situation occurred with the small German-speaking Pomeranian Slovincians, who after the war were first forcibly "Slavicised," "Polonised," "de-Germanised," and finally in the 1970s allowed to emigrate to West Germany (Filip 2018).

This kind of ethno-linguistic cleansing made Poland almost a fully mono-linguistic country in the early post-socialist years in the 1990s. Surviving minority languages were marginalized to provincial, non-prestigious dialects of the Polish language, or under social pressure, their use was limited to the family-home zone. The hermeticity of the post-war linguistic situation in Poland was reinforced by the border regime, under which cross-border mobility of citizens was limited to a minimum. All the processes mentioned above led to the nationalization of language, within which almost the absolute number of Polish language users was counted as part of the Polish national community as citizens of the Polish People's Republic or as members of the diaspora – the so-called Polonia. The liberalization of the border regime after 1989 and accession to the European Union in 2004 marked the end of the small stability of the socialist period and triggered mass mobility. Millions of Poles emigrated to Western Europe in search of well-paid jobs and better living standards. In their place, often filling the same professional niches as Poles in the UK and Germany, immigrants from post-socialist countries arrived. The nationalist linguistic utopia was disrupted, and Polish became a language learned by millions of migrants and refugees in various modes.

Transition to a free-market economy

Teaching Polish as a foreign language is intimately connected to political, economic, and migration processes. The most significant milestones include (1) the systemic transformation in Poland and the dissolution of the USSR (1989–1991), (2) Poland's accession to the EU, (3) the gradual opening of the labor market to citizens of Ukraine, Belarus, and other non-EU countries (from 2008), the Russian aggression against Ukraine (2014), and (5) the full-scale war in Ukraine and political repressions in Belarus (2020–2024). These processes have generated the main push factors causing migrants to leave their countries of origin and settle elsewhere, while pull factors attract migrants to Poland. A clear correlation between the dynamics of migration processes and Polish language teaching can be observed. In the 1990s and 2000s, Polish as a foreign language was primarily learned by people claiming Polish ancestry. With Poland's entry into the European Union and the increasing attractiveness of the Polish labor market, the role of economic migrants and educational migrants, for whom studies in Poland often constituted a form of legalizing their stay in the EU, increased.

Though spread over a quarter of a century, the changes can be considered cardinal, as they significantly transformed Polish society in cultural and linguistic terms. The Polish People's Republic has consistently formed a mono-ethnic and monolingual society for nearly half a century. It was achieved not only by mass expulsions of German, Ukrainian, and Jewish populations but also through the policy of assimilating ethnic and national minorities, standardizing the Polish language, and excluding minority languages from public space and education (Filip 2015: 167–170). Linguistic standardization was also facilitated by a special border regime characteristic of socialist bloc countries, where cross-border movement was limited and strictly controlled. As a result, by 1989, Polish was the first language for the overwhelming majority of Polish citizens. Due to the semi-peripheral position of the Polish People's Republic in the global economy, Polish did not become a language of international communication and was systematically taught as a second language among three groups: (1) Polish diaspora in former USSR, Western Europe and America, (2) students from the Third World and the socialist bloc who undertook studies in Poland, (3) a few Slavists, for whom Polish was usually an additional Slavic language.

The situation changed slightly after the liberalization of the border movement and systemic reforms at the turn of the 1980s and 1990s, when economic migrants, war refugees from (post-)socialist countries (Romania, Nagorno-Karabakh, Ukraine, Chechnya, Belarus, Vietnam), and Polish repatriates from the territories of the former USSR began to arrive in Poland (Hut, Żołądek 2013: 172–184). During this period, the main challenge was the school integration of migrant children, and the language education of adults was not given much attention. For people of Polish origin from the territories of the former USSR, the breakthrough years were 2007–2008, when new repatriation regulations were introduced, and the Polish Card – a document confirming affiliation with the Polish nation, based on which one can apply for an indefinite stay in the territory of the Republic of Poland, work permit, and also study for free at Polish public universities (Szonert, Łodziński 2016: 88) – began to be issued. Obtaining the Polish Card is preceded by an exam in the Polish language and history of Poland, for which candidates often prepare at special courses. Since 2008, more than 350,000 people (mainly in Ukraine and Belarus) have applied for this document, making the Polish Card an institution generating an entire infrastructure for learning the Polish language among people who can demonstrate Polish ancestry.

Further migration changes occurred in the following decades when a significant labor shortage appeared in the Polish market due to rapid economic growth and massive economic migrations of Poles to EU countries. Poland had to open up to immigration, but due to the social distance of the majority of citizens towards migrants from Muslim cultures, Polish authorities primarily targeted immigrants from neighboring Ukraine and Belarus (Buchowski 2020). The Polish labor market opened up to workers from Ukraine, Belarus, Armenia, Georgia,

Russia, and Moldova, which was legally expressed by the *Act on Foreigners* of 2013, which introduced a simplified procedure for employing workers from these countries (Szonert, Łodziński 2016: 38). Over time, market demands forced the opening up to immigrants from Asian countries: Nepal, India, Bangladesh, and others.

Refugees and economic migrants from Ukraine and Belarus

The simplified procedure allowed, in 2014, the smooth legalization and economic integration of war refugees from Ukraine without the need to initiate procedures related to granting refugee status. As a result of the above processes, in 2019, Poland was home to over 2,106,000 foreigners, of whom 64% were Ukrainians and 5% were Belarusians. The largest groups of foreigners were made up of people of working age (15–64 years), which constituted as much as 86% of all foreigners staying in Poland (GUS 2020: 12). This situation resulted in an increased demand for Polish language courses for adults, primarily aimed at economic migrants. The primary motivation for learning Polish among this group was to improve one's professional qualifications and the prospects of permanent settlement in Poland.

The number of migrants has created a demand for new forms of Polish language education aimed at children and adults. In 2016, the Ministry of National Education introduced preparatory classes in selected schools designed for students who need to learn Polish or whose language knowledge is insufficient for starting education. At this time, many private language schools also emerged, offering Polish language courses for foreigners. Non-governmental organizations involved in migrant integration launched free Polish language courses. Public universities also opened commercial education programs. Such courses are popular because a B1-level certificate of Polish language proficiency is required to apply for a permanent residence card or Polish citizenship. At the same time, we can observe the emergence of vocational post-secondary schools and higher education institutions preparing their educational offerings almost exclusively for immigrants from Ukraine, Belarus, and other post-Soviet countries. These schools have become institutions that legalize and specifically enculturate immigrants. Starting education is a convenient way to legalize one's stay in Poland.

The situation changed dramatically with the escalation of the political conflict in Belarus in 2020 and an outbreak of War in Ukraine in February 2022. Increased political repression in Belarus following the rigged presidential elections and mass protests in 2020 pushed a number of migrants and political refugees to Poland, and the full-scale war in Ukraine led to the most significant influx of refugees in Poland's post-war history. The war caused Europe's most enormous wave of migration since World War II, with over 5 million people leaving Ukraine only in the first three months. Poland became the leading destination country for Ukrainian refugees, offering them temporary protection, the right to work, access to education, and social assistance (Bloch, Szmyt 2024: 4–5). The Polish government's response to the refugee crisis was to introduce many facilitations for Ukrainian citizens, including the possibility of free Polish language courses. The courses are organized by public institutions, non-governmental organizations, and private language schools and are financed from public funds, European funds, and donations. The main goal of these courses is to facilitate the integration of refugees into Polish society and the labor market.

At the peak of war refugees from Ukraine in April 2022, more than 3 million refugees arrived in Poland, of which 1.5 million stayed in Poland for a more extended period. Under a special law, the Polish government introduced simplified procedures for legalizing Ukrainian refugees for 18 months. Upon receiving a PESEL number with a UKR annotation, refugees gained the right to work, healthcare, and social benefits. By the end of 2022, 949,381 PESEL numbers with the UKR annotation had been issued. Over 45% of these were minors, 48% were working age, and more than 6% were post-working age (Jarosz, Klaus 2023: 15–16). These were primarily people from eastern and southern Ukraine who had had no contact with the Polish language. Learning Polish became necessary for effective social integration in the labour market. The issue of non-school Polish language education concerns not only adult migrants but also children. In 2022, out of the 432,621 Ukrainian children in Poland, only 234,000 attended Polish schools and kindergartens (Ibidem: 31–33). The compulsory schooling for all long-term Ukrainian children residing in Poland will only come into force from September 2024 – two and a half years after the start of the war and the million-strong refugee immigration from Ukraine. The unexpected appearance of hundreds of thousands of underage refugees from Ukraine in Polish schools has brought a number of challenges for teachers not trained to work with Ukrainian and Russian-speaking children and has also sparked many conflicts involving Polish children and their parents concerned about the level of education in classes where some children do not have sufficient language skills (Tędziagolska, Walczak, Żelazowska-Kasiorek 2022: 24–41).

The remaining children were learning remotely in Ukrainian schools, so teaching these individuals Polish cannot be done within the Polish school system. The spontaneous self-organisation of Polish society to help refugees from Ukraine and pro-refugee actions by the government and local authorities resulted in an unprecedented increase in language courses for Ukrainians. Non-governmental organisations, local governments, companies, universities, and private individuals began organising more or less ephemeral forms of non-school linguistic education in remote and stationary forms.

In many cases, volunteers without experience or glottodidactic education become teachers. Teaching Polish to foreigners has become a widespread phenomenon, decentralised and increasingly organised from the grassroots level. The number of economic and political migrants from Ukraine and Belarus allows us to predict that in the coming years, more than 3 million foreigners staying in Poland will be learning Polish, most of whom are not subject to compulsory schooling or are fulfilling it remotely in their country of origin.

Conclusions

In migration studies, the acquisition of the language of the host society is considered a key determinant of successful immigrant integration. Planning Polish language teaching programs for migrants must take into account the most important elements of migratory structure and scenarios of newcomers. For several years, the Polish system of teaching Polish as a foreign language has been focused on stationary school and university education for a limited number of immigrants and Polish repatriates from the former USSR territories. Mass economic migration, political migration, as well as refugees from authoritarian Belarus and war-torn Ukraine, have been a game-changer. Existing forms of language education do not meet the needs of large migrant groups, such as working adults or post-productive age individuals. Polish schools were also unprepared to receive and organize education for hundreds of thousands of Ukrainian and Russian-speaking children from Ukraine. The language education of refugees in the early years of the war was conducted spontaneously and in an unorganized manner as a grassroots initiative by volunteers, NGOs, companies, and local authorities. So far, these initiatives have not been systematized, and the main problems include a lack of long-term funding for educational initiatives, a shortage of qualified staff, and a lack of channels for continuing education beyond the initial level of language proficiency – A1-A2. The effective implementation of integration policy for immigrants will depend on the ability of Polish state institutions to organize a system of school and extracurricular language education for children and adults, as well as on the effectiveness of coordinating teaching activities conducted by thousands of NGOs.

Bibliography

Beręsewicz M. et al., *Populacja cudzoziemców w Polsce w czasie COVID-19* (Badania eksperymentalne GUS), 2020, https://stat.gov.pl/statystyki-eksperymentalne/kapital-lud zki /populacja-cudzoziemcow-w-polsce-w-czasie-covid-19,12,1.html [accessed 20.10. 2023].

Bloch N., Szmyt Z. *Nomadland. Miejsca zbiorowego zakwaterowania osób uchodźczych z Ukrainy w Wielkopolsce a procesy integracyjne,* Poznań: Centrum Badań Migracyjnych UAM, 2024.

Buchowski M. *Distant vs. Familiar Significant Others: Attitudes towards Absent Muslim Refugees and Extant Labor Migrants in Poland*, "Asian Journal of Peacebuilding", 2020, 8:1, pp. 75–93.

Gellner E. Ernest. 1983. *Nations and Nationalism.* Oxford: Blackwell.

Filip M. *Dlaczego Słowińcy nie chcą rozmawiać? O antropologicznym czytaniu historii,* "Rocznik Antropologii Historii", 2015, 5(8), pp. 167–188.

Filip M. 2018, A tribe after all? The problem of Slovincians' identity in an anthropological approach, "Studia Slavica et Balcanica Petropolitana" 2 (24), s. 145–168.

Hut P., Żołądek Ł. 2013, (red.), *Repatrianci i polityka repatriacyjna,* "Studia BAS" 2(34).

Jarosz S., Klaus W. (red.) 2023, *Polska szkoła pomagania. Przyjęcie osób uchodźczych z Ukrainy w Polsce w 2022 roku,* Warszawa: Konsorcjum Migracyjne.

Łodziński S., Szonert M. *Polityka migracyjna w Polsce w latach 1989–2015,* w: J. Schmidt, D. Niedźwiedzki (eds.) Społeczno-kulturowa identyfikacja cudzoziemców Raporty i ekspertyzy, Poznań: Wydawnictwo Naukowe UAM, 2016, pp. 11–66.

Motyka G. 2023, From the Volhynian Massacre to Operation Vistula, Paderborn: Brill.

Phillipson R. 1992, Linguistic Imperialism. Oxford: Oxford University Press.

Stola D. 2007, Fighting against the Shadow w: R. Blobaum (red.) Antisemitism and Its Opponents in Modern Poland, Ithaca, London: Cornell University Press, s. 284–300.

Tędziagolska M., Walczak B., Żelazowska-Kasiorek A. 2022, Culturally diverse school Challenges and needs stemming from the arrival of Ukrainian students, Warsaw: The Center for Citizenship Education.

Yuliia Vaseiko / Natalia Tsolyk
(Lesya Ukrainka Volyn National University in Lutsk)

The state of teaching Polish as a foreign language in Ukraine after 2022

Abstract

This paper reviews the current state of teaching Polish as a foreign language in Ukraine in the social, systemic and institutional context. The analysis focuses on governmental laws and programs, teacher preparation and most utilized textbooks in order to establish the needs and challenges both for practice and research in PFL tuition in Ukraine.

Teaching Polish in Ukraine dates back to the 1990s, after the country gained independence. For three decades, the system, programs, forms and goals of teaching have been developing. These processes constitute the subject of research led by scientists from Poland and Ukraine. Attention has been given to issues such as qualified teaching staff and fundamental challenges in their work (Strutyński 2004). Efforts have been made to identify the most effective forms of teaching Polish (Chłopek 2009). Additionally, researchers have focused on regional aspects of teaching (Krasowska, Suchomłynow 2021; Zielińska 2011; Pelekhata 2022), and discussions have taken place regarding the motivation to learn Polish (Levchuk, Stapor 2022). The 1st World Congress of Polish Education and Science Abroad was held in July 2023, the aim of which was to "build the Polish educational community in the world, integrate Polish and Polish communities abroad, exchange the experiences of teachers and scientists working abroad, as well as develop substantive proposals and systemic solutions" (World Congress of Polish Education and Science Abroad. 2023).

Currently, in Ukraine, Polish language teaching takes place in units supervised by the Ministry of Education and Science of Ukraine or in entities not subject to supervision. The latter include Saturday-Sunday schools at Polish organizations and parishes, courses, foreign language schools, and offers of private teachers. There is a School Consultation Point at the Embassy of the Republic of Poland in Kiev, where students can obtain school certificates applicable under Polish education law.

According to information from the Ukrainian Ministry of Education and Science of Ukraine, Institute of Educational Analytics in Kiev, provided in the *Study Monitoring the Meeting of the Educational Needs of National Minorities in Educational Institutions*, the outbreak of war with Russia in 2022 resulted in a reduction in the number of people learning foreign languages in Ukrainian schools. The reason for this is migration processes – many families with school-age children have changed their place of residence, and people in occupied areas have limited educational opportunities. However, the interest among students in learning in Polish or teaching Polish as a foreign language has increased:

> Over the last five years, the number of students who study Polish or teach the Polish language in general secondary schools has increased by 29.2% (from 80,070 in the 2018/2019 school year to 103,456 students in the 2022/2023 school year). (Моніторингове дослідження щодо задоволення освітніх потреб національних меншин у закладах освіти 2023)

Data from the Ministry of Education and Science of Ukraine show that in the 2020–2021 school year, most schools where students learned Polish were in the Lviv, Volyn, Ivano-Frankivsk, Zhytomyr, Rivne regions (Освіта польської національн ої меншини в Україні: стан і перспективи розвитку 2021). In 2023, the situation has not changed. Only in Lutsk schools in 2023/2023, according to official data of the Volyn Regional Education Board, 12,966 students learn Polish.

The rising popularity and growing prestige of the Polish language are apparent, as indicated by the Ukrainian office's contemplation of the potential inclusion of the Polish language examination among the subjects eligible for independent external evaluation:

> We need to take specific actions to integrate with the European space. The first step is to teach the languages of neighboring countries. This step should be mutual: Poles are ready to include Ukrainian as a foreign language on the list of school subjects. At the same time, the Ukrainian side should develop a strategy for passing Polish language exams. And if this requires changes in regulations, this process must be started today (Верещук 2023).

Statistical data confirm that the Polish language is exceptionally popular among students of Ukrainian secondary schools. There are many reasons for this. First of all, it is easy to teach this language. There are many similarities with the Ukrainian language at various levels, especially in terms of vocabulary, phonetics and even grammar. The Polish alphabet does not discourage learners, because most of them have already had contact with English or German, i. e. alphabets based on the Latin alphabet. Geographical, political and cultural reasons also contribute to the popularization of the Polish language. Poland is one of Ukraine's closest neighbors, an EU country, a NATO member, it presents high living standards, a good education system, wide employment opportunities, and is not too mentally different, which encourages parents and students to choose Polish among other foreign languages.

In recent years, there have been changes in the Polish language teaching system in Ukraine due to the fact that since 2018, a key reform of the Ministry of Education and Science of Ukraine has been implemented in the country – the New Ukrainian School (NUS), the aim of which is:

> Comprehensive development, education and formation of individuals who perceive themselves as citizens of Ukraine, capable of living in the society and interacting with nature in a civilized way, aspire for self-perfection and life-long study, are ready for a conscious life choice and self-fulfillment, labor activities and community involvement (The New Ukrainian school Conceptual principles of secondary School reform 2016).

The process of implementing the reform is regulated by the following laws, resolutions and regulations: *The New Ukrainian school Conceptual principles of secondary School reform* (2016), *The Act on Education* (2017), *The State Standard of Primary Education* (2018), *The State Standard of Basic Secondary Education* (2020) etc.

The education reform provides for 12 years of education: primary school – 1–4 grades (4 years); primary secondary school (middle schools) – 5–9 grades (5 years); specialized secondary school (high schools: general and vocational) – 10–12 grades (3 years).

The NUS concept introduces changes to the teaching programs, including foreign languages, including Polish. We will consider what changes have occurred in teaching Polish in Ukrainian schools in the context of NUS in primary secondary schools.

At NUS there is no division into subjects, but there are different fields of education: linguistic and literary (Polish was included as a second foreign language), mathematical, technical, etc. For each field, a common goal for all levels of the school and competence potential are defined, i. e. the ability to shape key competences (including communication in foreign languages) through the development of skills and acquisition of basic knowledge.

The aim of the linguistic and literary field is:

> Development of competent speakers and readers with a humanistic worldview, speaking Ukrainian, reading information and artistic texts, including classical and contemporary literature (Ukrainian and world), able to communicate in the native language and national minorities, foreign languages for the very purpose of national and cultural expression, for conducting intercultural dialogue, for enriching emotional experience, creative self-fulfillment, shaping the system of human values (Державний стандарт базової середньої освіти 2020).

The requirements for mandatory learning outcomes in the linguistic and literary field (including teaching Polish as a foreign language) provide that the student:

Receives oral and written texts in a foreign language in conditions of direct and indirect intercultural communication; interacts with other people orally and in writing using a foreign language; provides information, expresses thoughts and feelings in a foreign language (Державний стандарт базової середньої освіти 2020).

From September 1, 2022, the principles of NUS are implemented in 5 grades of primary secondary school. In 2023/2024 the principles of NUS are introduced in grades 5 and 6, respectively. As of September 1, 2021, some schools started implementing the NUS program in experimental classes in which students started learning according to NUS requirements a year earlier (e.g. Lutsk Secondary School No. 1).

According to the model curriculum, starting from the 5th grade, students are expected to choose a second foreign language, including Polish, which they learn two hours a week. "The choice of language is made taking into account objective and subjective factors: availability of staff, capabilities of educational institutions, desires of students" (Редько В. Г., Шаленко О. П. et al. 2021).

The content of teaching a second foreign language should include, among others:

Comprehensive mastery of all language activities (listening, speaking, reading, writing), concentricity of the presentation of educational materials, situational justification of exercises and tasks; implementing a cultural approach into the teaching process by using tasks modeling situations of communicative interaction in accordance with the principles of cultural dialogue; creating a communicative atmosphere during lessons, bringing it closer to the conditions of authentic communication, ensuring the possibility of multi-channel communicative interaction by performing various exercises and tasks individually, in pairs and in groups, depending on social communication needs; performing tasks of an action-oriented, problem-oriented, creative nature, developing creative thinking, general education skills, conscious use of one's own educational experience, including in the field of learning the mother tongue and the first foreign language (Редько В. Г., Шаленко О. П. et al. .2021).

Authors of the curriculum *Second Foreign Language. Grades 5–9* for general secondary schools emphasize that the content of learning a second foreign language, including Polish, should:

Match the student's current communicative interest; stimulate the development of students' interests and positive attitude towards a second foreign language; aim to engage students both in a language code that is new to them and in the culture of the nation; be based on students' experience in mastering their native language and first foreign language, consider students' general educational experiences acquired while teaching other subjects (Редько В. Г., Шаленко О. П. et al. 2021).

The process of teaching foreign languages, including Polish, at NUS is methodologically based on *Recommendation of the European Parliament and of the Council of 18 December 2006 on key competences for lifelong learning* and

Common European Framework of Reference for Languages: Learning, Teaching, Assessment.

The educational process in Polish as a foreign language lessons is based on a communicative, action and cultural approach. Since students learn Polish as a second foreign language, the teaching process considers the mother tongue system and the principles of acquiring the first foreign language, most often English, less often German or French, i.e. the phenomenon of positive and negative language transfers.

The process of teaching Polish in 5–6 classes, implementing the principles of NUS, is based on the model curriculum *Second Foreign Language. Grades 5–9.* for general secondary schools by V. Redko, O. Shalenko, S. Sotnikova, O. Kovalenko, I. Koropetska, O. Jacob, I. Samoilukevich, O. Dobra, T. Kior, M. Mackovich, L. Hlyniuk, E. Brown and manuals by M. Mackovich, R. Tseselska-Musameg, K. Kviatkovska: *Polish language (first year of teaching, second foreign language)* and *Polish language (second year of teaching, second foreign language)* recommended by the Ministry of Education and Science of Ukraine. What is particularly important in war conditions, electronic versions of these textbooks are posted on the official website of the Institute for the Modernization of Education Content, from where they can be downloaded. A set of teaching aids for children and teenagers called Step by Step Junior 1, 2 by I. Stempek, P. Grudzien, P. Kuc is very popular among Ukrainian teachers.

Teachers who teach Polish in grades 7–11 or on an optional basis use programs and textbooks previously recommended by the Ministry of Education and Science of Ukraine. Program dla ogólnokształcących szkół średnich 5–9 klasy *Polish language* by O. Voitseva, T. Buchatska (2017 r.), program for general secondary schools with Ukrainian as the language of instruction *Polish language 10–11 grades. Standard level* (2017), textbooks Polish language for various grades by L. Bilenka-Svistovych, J. Kovalevski, M. Yarmoliuk and authors O. Voitseva, T. Buchatska, textbook for grade 11 in schools with in-depth study of foreign languages and general secondary schools *Polish language (Year 7, standard level)* by B. Guziuk-Switza, G. Przechodzka, A. Rochniak, M. Zielińska (2019) et al.

There are schools in the Lviv, Khmelnytsky and Ivano-Frankivsk oblasts where teaching is conducted in Polish. For such schools, the Ministry of Education and Science of Ukraine recommends appropriate programs: Program for general secondary schools with teaching in Polish, *Polish language. 6–9 grades* by M. Ivanov, N. Dutkevich, L. Gandz, M. Zielińska; curriculum *Polish language. Grades 5–9 (with teaching in Polish)* for general secondary schools by M. Ivanov et al. and textbooks for the 1st grade of general secondary schools with teaching in Polish (in 2 parts) *Polish language. Textbook*; for the 4th grade of general secondary schools with teaching in Polish, *Polish language and reading* by R. Lebed, I. Slobodian et al.

According to information from the Ukrainian Ministry of Education and Science of Ukraine, Institute of Educational Analytics in Kiev, provided in the *Study Monitoring the Meeting of the Educational Needs of National Minorities in Educational Institutions:* "the first places in terms of the number of textbooks recommended by the Ministry of Education and Science of Ukraine are held by materials in Hungarian (21, 1%) and Polish (18.1%)". (Моніторингове дослідження щодо задоволення освітніх потреб націо нальних menshin у закладах освіти 2023).

Polish language teachers in general secondary schools are mainly graduates of Polish studies from Ukrainian universities. The Ministry of Education and Science of Ukraine in the presentation *Education of the Polish national minority in Ukraine:* status and prospects states that 13 universities educate Polish teachers in the following fields: 014 Teachers and 035 Philology, namely the Drohobych State Pedagogical University, the Volhynian National University. Lesya Ukrainka, State University of Ivan Franko in Zhytomyr, Precarpathian National University named after Wasyl Stefanyk, Ternopil National Pedagogical University. Volodymyr Hnatyuk, Khmelnytsky National University, Kyiv National Linguistic University, Kyiv National University. Taras Shevchenko, Lviv National University. Ivan Franko et al. The number of such students is increasing: 2020 – 606, 2021 – 858 тан та perspectivi розвитку 2021).

The increasing interest in the Polish language among high school graduates is evidenced by the increase in the number of students in the 1st year of Polish Studies at the Volhynian National University named after Lesia Ukrainka in Lutsk, where 27 students studied in the 2020/2021 academic year, 2022/2023. – 39, 2023/2024 – 45. The number of students studying teaching is also increasing: 2021/2022 – 16, 2022/2023 – 20, 2023/2024 – 26. Which is also largely dependent on state support. Every year, studies for 15 students are financed from the state budget. What is important is the fact that after these studies, graduates of Polish studies in Lutsk have no problems finding a job in both state schools and private educational institutions.

Professional education of students as future teachers and lecturers of the Polish language is carried out within the framework of basic and specialized education subjects: *Methodology of teaching the Polish language, Polish linguistics teaching, Methodology of teaching Polish literature, Methodology of teaching Slavic languages,* etc., and within free-choice subjects in the field of Polish language teaching. as a foreign language, methodology of teaching Polish literature: *Information and communication technologies as modern tools for teaching Polish, Pedagogical grammar, Certificate examination in Polish as a foreign language* (Volyn National University named after Lesya Ukrainka), *Methodology of teaching Polish literature in higher education, Methods of using games in teaching (on the example of the Polish language), Methodology of teaching Polish as a foreign language* (Ivan Franko National University of Lviv) and others. The course syllabi are practical, considering the content and tasks of modern PFL learning methods and programs, the requirements of the NUS, as well as the regional conditions of their implementation. For example, the course *Methodology of teaching Polish at the Volhynian National University* named after Lesia Ukrainka provides the following topics: from the benefits of knowing foreign languages, types and levels of knowing a foreign language, the goals of learning foreign languages, motivation for learning foreign languages, the history of shaping methods of learning foreign languages to the achievements of Polish language glottodidactics, the history of learning Polish as a foreign language in the world and in Ukraine, teaching Polish under the conditions of the NUS. This program focuses on the personality of a Polish language teacher, on distance and inclusive teaching, the causes of students' school failures and the principles of their correction during teaching, methods of assessing students' work during Polish language lessons, various forms of activities of a Polish language teacher conducive to an integrated, holistic perception by teachers. PFL of Polish culture, including knowledge about Poland, its history, culture, intercultural teaching methodologies, and multilingualism didactics.

During the classes, prospective Polish language teachers engage in discussions on various aspects of the teaching process in Ukraine. These include the legal principles governing education, as well as the examination of programs and textbooks designed for teaching Polish in schools. Additionally, they explore guidelines for utilizing audiovisual materials and the Internet in lessons. Techniques for acquiring grammatical, lexical, and semantic knowledge are also covered. The learning process extends to the development of linguistic competences, oral reception skills, reading comprehension, and proficiency in oral production and interaction. Learning this material will allow you to accomplish the basic tasks of this course – to teach future teachers of Polish:

> Developing students' key and subject competences, implementing in practice a communicative, action-oriented and intercomprehensive approach when teaching Polish, effective forms and methods of learning phonetics, spelling, morphology, syntax, word formation, working with text, methods of presenting tourist material (Ю. Васейко, Н. Mikhalyuk 2023).

The basis for developing these courses are the works of Polish scientists W. Miodunka, P. Gębal, A. Seretna, Z. Chłopek, P. Levchuk, H. Komarowska, J. Kowalewski and others. Ukrainian educators also intensively join in discussing important issues in the field of teaching Polish as a foreign language during numerous conferences, seminars, in their articles and textbooks (L. Bilenka-Svistovych, A. Chłopek, L. Hlyniuk, A. Kravchuk, M. Mackovich, Y. Vaseiko, O. Voitseva, N. Tsolyk, M. Zielińska et al.). Every year, the International Scientific and Didactic Panel on the *State and Prospects of Polish Language Teaching in Secondary and Higher Education* is held at the Volyn National University named after Lesia Ukrainka, in which Polish and Ukrainian scientists, lecturers and teachers of the Polish language, and students take part. The fourth panel took place this year. Polish studies in Ukraine are eager to join international projects of Polish universities financed by NAWA (*Improvement of linguistic, cultural and didactic competences of Ukrainian teachers of Polish as a foreign language, GLOTTOPOL – Didactics of Polish as a Foreign Language against the European Background. Publication and training package, Grammar of culture – webinars and tasks*, etc.), which serves to exchange experience more effectively, expand glottodidactic knowledge, etc.

Ukrainian teachers of Polish as a foreign language develop their professional qualifications, expand their glottodidactic knowledge by taking part in teacher development programs offered by the Union of Polish Teachers in Ukraine, the Khmelnytsky Regional Institute of Postgraduate Pedagogical Studies, the Volhynian Institute of Postgraduate Pedagogical Studies and other institutions in order to improve the methodological and practical professional competences of Polish language teachers.

Polish language teacher development programs provide for the development and implementation of general topics related to the state education development strategy, basic teacher competencies, and the requirements of the NUS.

However, the detailed content concerns the methodology of teaching Polish in the conditions of the NUS, expands teachers' knowledge about the competence approach in teaching Polish, modeling a modern Polish language lesson and assessing students' achievements, modern methodologies for developing linguistic, socio-cultural and sociolinguistic competences of students, etc. Ukrainian teachers actively participate in international projects and webinars conducted by Polish specialists. For example, the GLOSSA Polish Language School offers paid and free methodological courses, webinars and training. They are very popular among Ukrainian teachers because they are based on the *Step by Step* series of textbooks. In addition to practical advice and tips on how to work with the book, participants gain skills in working with the e-polish.eu educational platform and receive discounts on the purchase of methodological aids, games, and Polish language learning kits. In 2023, the *Samodzielność od Kuchni* foundation organized a number of free training courses for teachers "Polish language as a foreign language with an emotional regulation component". After completing the course, participants received certificates, a package of JPJO textbooks and a discount on all textbooks available in the bookstore at *startpolish.pl*.

Graduates of Ukrainian Polish studies work not only as teachers, but also as translators, employees of state authorities, diplomatic missions, private companies, etc. They receive the necessary knowledge and skills while developing the content of the subjects *Contemporary Polish Language, Theory and Practice of Translation, Culture and Stylistics of the Polish Language,* etc. In 2019, the Ministry of Education and Science of Ukraine approved and implemented the Standard of Higher Education of Ukraine in the specialty "Philology" for the first (bachelor's) educational level. On its basis, changes were introduced to the study programs, including an increase in internships to 24 ECTS points. Regulating the requirements, competences and educational results allows you to achieve the teaching goal:

> Education of specialists capable of solving complex specialized tasks and practical problems in the field of philology, characterized by complexity and uncertainty of conditions, namely in activities related to the analysis, creation (including translation) and evaluation of written and oral texts of various genres and styles, organization of successful communication in different languages. (Стандарт вищої освіти України за спеціальністю «Філологія» для пе ршого (бакалаврського) рівня вищої освіти 2019)

Students from the catalog of free-choice disciplines can add subjects they consider necessary to their study plan. If a graduate of philology wants to work at a school, according to the requirements of NUS, he or she does not have to have a pedagogical education. Such a young teacher will be assigned a teacher-mentor who will support the first steps in the profession.

Not only students of Polish studies at Ukrainian universities learn Polish. The subjects: "Polish language course", "Polish language (as a foreign language)", "Theory and practice of translation", "Business communication in foreign languages" are included in the education programs of students of International Relations, Ukrainian Studies, History and others. The "Double Diploma" program, which provides for joint teaching of Ukrainian students at Polish universities at the same time, resulted in the need for students of Medicine, Ecology, Cultural Studies, etc. to have good knowledge of the Polish language.

There is a growing demand among university candidates for fields of study that allow them to master several foreign languages. This type of education for Polish teachers was proposed in the early 2000s:

> Educating a student from Ukraine solely to become a Polish language teacher is a waste of time. It seems necessary to simultaneously prepare a young person to work as a teacher in other subjects (Ukrainian, English, etc.). Such a system would favor the employment of graduates in Ukrainian schools and would enable the spread of Polish language classes. Ukrainian youth from Poland studying at universities in Ukraine should be educated similarly. (Strutyński 2004)

This allows to get a better job in the future without leaving the region. In the years 2022–2023, the number of students studying Polish studies, specializing in 035 Philology, has doubled. The Volyn Oblast shares a common state border with the Republic of Poland, over two hundred kilometers long, which facilitates the region's participation in the implementation of Polish-Ukrainian cross-border cooperation programs. Lutsk, the regional center of Volhynia, is the twin city of six Polish partners. Therefore, the demand for philologists ensuring communication at all levels of international exchange is growing every year.

It was commonly believed that Polish was taught as the native language in Saturday-Sunday schools attached to Polish organizations or parishes. Unfortunately, in Ukraine the actual situation does not always correspond to this postulate. In the early 1990s, after the revival of the church, Poles began to create Polish organizations and Polish language schools within them. People aged 6 to 90 started learning the language. Seniors spoke Polish (they read and wrote worse), and young people and middle-aged people did not have communication skills. The long years of Soviet reality, when parents did not teach their children Polish at home because they were afraid of persecution (especially in Volhynia) – led to generations of Poles who did not speak Polish. Teaching during this period was very chaotic: there were no curricula for diverse groups, no textbooks, no qualified teachers, and no acceptance by local authorities.

After years of support from compatriots abroad, the situation in Polish schools in Ukraine has improved. Organizations – the "Wspólnota Polska" Association, the Help for Poles in the East Foundation, the Freedom and Democracy Foundation – offered participation in projects thanks to which it was possible to obtain equipment, textbooks, methodological aids, costs for the purchase of furniture and renovation, organize summer camps and study stays. The Center for the Development of Polish Education Abroad (ORPEG) was established, and with it the possibility of sending teachers from Poland to work in Polish schools.

There was a need to systematize Polish language teaching institutions in Ukraine. The Platform of Good Practices was created by the Freedom and Democracy Foundation. In addition to materials for teachers (lesson plans, presentations, textbooks), there is also information about Polish studies and language courses in Ukraine. In 2018, the Geopolonistyka project was launched:

> A world map showing the locations of former and current Polish studies centers around the world. This solution is based on the integration of several types of content included in the "Polish Philology Bulletin": a database, information texts and an interactive OpenStreetMap map enabling geolocation. Linking the map with articles and the database also allows us to present the profiles of scientists conducting research on Polish literature, culture and language, and, as a result, present the state of research on Polish literature outside the country as well as information about the present and history of all institutions conducting Polish studies in the world. (*O geopolonistyce* 2018)

Information about Polish and Polish diaspora schools can be obtained from the ORPEG website. For several years, a school applying for any support has been obliged to register (annually update) data in the Polish School / School Database system. From 2022, each organization applying for funding must be included in the Central Statistical Office register of Polish and Polish organizations abroad. It should be mentioned that Ukrainian and Polish studies schools have also been included in these registers, as they have the opportunity to apply for support. In fact, at this level the boundaries between the school in the Ukrainian educational system and the Polish school are blurring.

Using the example of a school operating at the Tadeusz Kościuszko Polish Culture Society in Łuck in Volhynia, we will describe the state of teaching Polish and the basic problems. The advantages of working in a Polish school include the freedom to choose the curriculum and textbooks (the lack of restrictions allows them to be adapted to each group). Every year, teachers delegated by ORPEG work at the school and provide consultations on the latest textbooks, programs, training for teachers, etc. The school permanently employs four teachers – graduates of Ukrainian universities. They are also members of the Union of Polish Teachers in Ukraine, which brings together "teachers of the Polish language and subjects taught in Polish in kindergartens, secondary schools, universities and out-of-school institutions." (Platform of Good Practices 2017) The biggest challenge is the division of people willing to learn Polish, about 200 people, into groups: firstly, the level of language knowledge must be considered (Polish schools are often attended by students who learn Polish in Ukrainian schools, and after 2022 – those who returned from Poland) secondly, the age of the student is important (from 6 to 80+ years). Groups of different ages and levels are most often formed. Classes are held in two shifts (morning and afternoon) on weekdays from October to June. A basic Polish language teaching course designed for three years. During the first year, reading and writing/printing skills in Polish are developed. Vocabulary is taught based on typical communication situations, and grammar issues are developed in the form of games. Subsequent years of study deepen knowledge, for those interested there are additional classes on Polish history, knowledge about Poland, physics (in Polish). Since 2020, teachers delegated from Poland have been conducting classes remotely (this was caused by the pandemic and then the war). The number of students at school after 2022 has not decreased. Only the teaching mode changed: classes were conducted remotely via Skype or Zoom. From spring 2023, teaching will be conducted in a mixed mode (in school classrooms, remotely). In the event of a threat during an alarm, students and teachers go to the shelter, and in the event of a power outage, a generator is connected. Changes are being observed in the purpose of teaching the language. Before the war, it was a preparation for submitting documents for the Pole's Card or studying in Poland. After 2022, the number of people interested in continuing school education in Poland from the 9th grade has increased. Polish schools also gained the opportunity to send students to the secondary school leaving examinations in order to obtain a Polish school certificate. Polish non-governmental organizations offered scholarships for such students.

Despite hostilities in Ukraine, after 2022 there have been positive changes in the system of teaching Polish as a foreign language. The concept of NUS envisages teaching Polish as a second foreign language in schools in Ukraine. The previous treatment of it as a national minority language did not correspond to the actual situation in schools, because Polish classes were attended by students of different nationalities. The number of people interested in learning Polish at various levels of education – from schools to universities – has increased. The need for distance learning (around the world it disappeared after the pandemic ended, and in Ukraine it was prolonged during the war for the following years) led to the creation of online platforms for students and teachers.

The system of teaching Polish as a foreign language in Ukraine, as well as every teaching process, is a dynamic process, responding to changes taking place in the life of society, requiring new approaches, techniques and didactic methodologies in teaching foreign languages, therefore this topic requires constant monitoring and analysis.

Bibliography

Baza danych szkół. [online:] https://www.orpeg.pl/db/web/database/baza-danych-szkol (02.02.2024).

Chłopek, A., *Zarys szkolnictwa polskiego na Ukrainie.* 2009 [online:] https://bazhum.m uzhp.pl/media/files/Postscriptum_Polonistyczne/Postscriptum_Polonistyczne-r2009- t-n1(3)/Postscriptum_Polonistyczne-r2009-t-n1(3)-s303-313/Postscriptum_Polonistyc zne-r2009-t-n1(3)-s303-313.pdf (02.02.2024).

Krasowska, H., Suchomłynow, L. A., *Stan oświaty polskiej w Charkowskim Okręgu Konsularnym.* 2021 [online:] file:///C:/Users/N/Downloads/artykuł%20polska/Stan_oświa ty_polskiej_w_Charkowskim.pdf (02.02.2024).

Levchuk, P., Stapor M. E., *Nauczanie języka polskiego jako obcego i odziedziczonego na Ukrainie i w Norwegii. Zarys problematyki.* 2022 [online:] https://web.archive.org/web /20220808163209id_/http://ddpu-filolvisnyk.com.ua/uploads/arkhiv-nomerov/2022/N V_2022_17/11.pdf (02.02.2024).

O Geopolonistyce. [online:] https://biuletynpolonistyczny.pl/pl/geoabout/ (02.02.2024).

Pelekhata, O., *Status języka polskiego wśród uczniów uczących się w klasach z językiem polskim jako językiem nauczania (na przykładzie Iwano-frankiwska, Ukraina).* 2022 [online:] http://www.poradnikjezykowy.uw.edu.pl/wydania/poradnik_jezykowy.799.2 022.10.11_Pelekhata.pdf (02.02.2024).

Platforma dobrych praktyk. [online:] https://platformadobrychpraktyk.wid.org.pl (02.02. 2024).

Platforma nr 1 dla uczących się i nauczających języka polskiego. https://e-polish.eu/polski -dla-obcokrajowcow (02.02.2024).

Strutyński, W., *Polska oświata na Ukrainie*. 2004 [online:] https://zbc.uz.zgora.pl/repozyto rium/Content/58875/19_strutynski_polska.pdf (02.02.2024).

Światowy Kongres Edukacji i Nauki Polskiej za Granicą. 2023 [online:] https://irjp.gov.pl /kongres2023/index.php (02.02.2024).

The New Ukrainian school Conceptual principles of secondary School reform, 2016 [online:] (https://mon.gov.ua/storage/app/media/zagalna%20serednya/Book-ENG.pdf) (27.01. 2024).

Zielińska, M., *Rola polszczyzny w życiu młodych użytkowników języka polskiego na Ukrainie Zachodniej*. 2021 [online:] https://repozytorium.amu.edu.pl/server/api/core/bi tstreams/088100f9-9133-46a9-b8de-bb97dce18bf2/content (02.02.2024).

Васейко, Ю., Михалюк, Н., *Силабус освітнього компонента "Методика навчання польської мови"*, підготовки бакалавра, галузі знань 01 Освіта /Педагогіка, спеціальності 014 Середня освіта (Польська мова та зарубіжна література), освітньо-професійної програми Середня освіта. Польська та англійська мови. Зарубіжна література, Луцьк 2023 [online:] https://drive.google.com/file/d/10G2mdchhMOq70c MrRjv8ihPBSYTz1MlR/view (28.01.2024).

Верещук І. *Освіта – один з інструментів інтеграції у Європейський прості*, 31.01.2023 [online:] https://www.kmu.gov.ua/news/iryna-vereshchuk-osvita-odyn-z-instrumenti v-intehratsii-u-ievropeiskyi-prostir (27.01.2024).

Державний стандарт базової середньої освіти, 2020 [online:] https://zakon.rada.gov.ua /laws/show/898-2020-%D0%BF#Text (27.01.2024).

Моніторингове дослідження щодо задоволення освітніх потреб національних меншин у закладах освіти, Міністерство освіти і науки України, ДНУ «Інститут освітньої аналітики» 2023 [online:] https://iea.gov.ua/wp-content/uploads/2023/12/nacz.mensh yny_2023.pdf (27.01.2024).

Освіта польської національної меншини в Україні: стан і перспективи розвитку. *Міністерство Освіти і науки України*, 2021 [online:] https://mon.gov.ua/storage/app /media/news/2021/01.11/2610-ukr.pdf (27.01.2024).

Редько, В., Шаленко, О., Сотникова, С., Коваленко, О., Коропецька, І., Якоб, О., Самойлюкевич, І., Добра, О., Кіор, Т., Мацькович, М., Глинюк Л., Браун, Є., *"Модельна навчальна програма Друга іноземна мова. 5–9 класи» для закладів загальної середньої освіти"*, 2021 [online:] https://mon.gov.ua/storage/app/media/zagalna%20serednya/Na vchalni.prohramy/2021/14.07/Model.navch.prohr.5-9.klas.NUSH-poetap.z.2022/Inozem ni.movy.5-9-kl/Druha.inoz.mov.5-9-kl.Redko.ta.in.14.07 (27.01.2024).

Стандарт вищої освіти України за спеціальністю «Філологія» для першого (бакалаврського) рівня вищої освіти 2019. [online:] http://fif.mdu.edu.ua/wp-content/up loads/2018/01/Стандарт-вищої-освіти-035-Філологія-БАКАЛАВР.pdf (03.02.2024).

Karol Krzyżosiak (University of Gdańsk)

Polish language among Ukrainians in the face of war in Ukraine. A transdisciplinary approach[1]

Abstract

The aim of this paper is to introduce a transdisciplinary approach applied to examine the migrant knowledge, linguistic biographies, learning beliefs, and subjective theories within the Ukrainian community learning Polish amidst migration contexts. This research endeavors to map the strategies and practices adopted by learners, analyzing the underlying thought patterns. By transcending disciplinary boundaries encompassing anthropology, applied linguistics and glottodidactics, this study seeks to offer a more nuanced and holistic perspective on the phenomena associated with learning Polish by Ukrainian migrants and refugees.

Introduction

In the face of war in Ukraine and the resulting multi-million mobility of refugees crossing Polish borders, the institutionalized education system has lost monopoly on the creation and distribution of methods of teaching Polish as a foreign language (PFL). We are observing a historical change in the status of the Polish language itself: from a local language, Polish is becoming a gateway language between the East and the West (Levchuk 2020). This change visibly affects the perception of the importance of learning Polish among Eastern Slavs. While in recent years Polish has become a prestigious language, enabling social advancement, in the face of war it is primarily a competence necessary to assure basic living conditions, as well as the possibility of settlement and employment. The growing demand for teaching PFL creates space for strategies and solutions that, although far from traditional school experiences, can be considered effective substitutes for formal language education. Polish state institutions were not prepared for the inflow of nearly 4 million people with refugee experience and

---

1 This article is the result of research conducted as part of the project titled "Mapping of new agents and tendencies in tuition of Polish as a foreign language among Ukrainian immigrants in Poland", implemented under the NAWA Intervention Grant BPN/GIN/2022/1/00088.

they could not organize and provide appropriate education on such a short notice, considering all the linguistic and psychopedagogical aspects important for such a demand. Therefore, initiatives for teaching Polish in the new, unknown reality were undertaken by many formal and informal entities, including non-governmental organizations, local and provincial governments, non-institutional volunteers, companies, reception centers and private individuals. All these grassroots initiatives were not systematically coordinated in terms of planning and organization, because in Poland, unlike Western countries, systemic solutions for linguistic and cultural education in the context of migration have never been created. An ad hoc, chaotic educational situation emerged, which generated a whole range of new educational contexts and processes. They require urgent identification (mapping) and focus on individual entities conducting classes, as well as categorization of a new type of learner and the methods and techniques of educational work being used. Only then will it be possible to substantively and organizationally coordinate governmental and non-governmental language education centers and develop effective, integration-friendly teaching approaches and program solutions for teaching Polish as a foreign and second language to new members of Polish society.

Given the problem posed in this way, acquiring knowledge that can constitute the basis for undertaking appropriate pedagogical and didactic activities is, above all, an epistemological challenge. Recognizing the complexity of relations between migration and education has important implications both for research and practice (Pamuła-Behrens M., Hennel-Brzozowska 2019). Indeed, migration affecting the entire society, marked by war trauma and anxiety about living conditions in the context of linguistic and cultural integration, encourages – not to say "forces" – the use of eclectic research tools. Therefore, we believe that a transdisciplinary approach to the presented problem is justified (Kita 2012), considering the methodological achievements of cultural anthropology and linguistic anthropology (Ahearn 2017) and migration studies (Williams 2007) on the one hand, and sociolinguistics, psycholinguistics and didactics of Polish as a foreign language on the other.

The purpose of this article is to introduce methodological solutions proposed as part of the ongoing NAWA intervention grant, titled "Mapping new agents and tendencies in tuition Polish as a foreign language among Ukrainian immigrants in Poland". They include four cognitive spaces such as "migrant knowledge" (Rajaram 2022), "linguistic biography" (Thoma 2022), "language learning beliefs" (White 2008), "subjective theories" (Michońska-Stadnik 2013) included in two interdisciplinary research categories: interpretative paradigm and process paradigm in field research (Buliński 2014). Within these categories, a concept of a new, specialized research area will be proposed, focused on the study of culturally entangled linguistic behaviors and activities on the Internet, which we call: *netnolinguistics*.

Methodological transdisciplinarity

Transdisciplinarity in the humanities is an integrative approach that transcends traditional disciplinary boundaries to address complex issues and challenges related to human behavior, society, and culture. Transdisciplinarity is not a model in itself – it is rather a property of a given methodological model or approach. Based on dialogue between various disciplines, such as: anthropology, linguistics, glottodidactics and psychology of learning in this case, transdisciplinary methodology strives for a comprehensive understanding of human phenomena. A key tenet of transdisciplinarity is the recognition that human systems are inextricably interconnected and that their study requires a multiperspective research (Paltridge 2020). A transdisciplinary approach emphasizes the importance of context, which encourages the synthesis of knowledge from various fields in order to thoroughly understand issues related to human behavior, practices and identity against the background of broader social dynamics. In practice, transdisciplinarity promotes a nuanced understanding of the multifaceted nature of the humanities, leading to innovative solutions to real-world problems.

Objects of study – operational definitions

Migrant knowledge

In the context of language learning, migrant knowledge is an overarching conceptual category encompassing both the biographies of learners as well as shared practices and beliefs. Its' scope is, of course, much broader, ranging from basic information about traveling to the country, through means of transport, prices, public places, discounts, social programs, to issues related to culture and entertainment. It is a collective and networked resource of experiences, observations and information co-created and shared by migrants in order to function more efficiently in a foreign country (Williams 2007).

In the context of migration, four types of knowledge (Sułkowski, Przytuła, Migdał 2020) can be discerned in order to purposefully orient the focus of both quantitative and qualitative studies:

1. *Embrained* – conceptual and cognitive skills, which give the opportunity to reflect on hidden meanings.

2. *Embodied* – produced as a result of practical experience, such as being in a given workplace; involves learning by doing.
3. *Encultured* – the common understanding of meanings, produced in the process of socialization and acculturation.
4. *Embedded* – context, produced as part of language systems, organizational cultures, groups, etc.

It can be assumed that especially 1., 3. and 4. are necessarily connected with language and the cultural meanings it carries. However, given the embodied nature of language learning, 2. should also be considered an important factor that constitutes migrant linguistic knowledge and plays a significant role in its transfer. One might consider, for instance, practices and strategies adapted by Ukrainians in acquiring and teaching phonetic skills. In particular, the aspects of teaching Polish pronunciation can be thoroughly studied thanks to the internet, as numerous online tutors and content creators offer insights in proper ways of articulating Polish sounds.

Migrant knowledge is disseminated both through direct interactions and through social media: YouTube channels, Facebook groups, Tik-Tok videos, Instagram posts and stories, blogs, etc. In the context of learning Polish as a foreign language, the first category includes practical advice and exchange of experiences. One of my interlocutors recalls, for example, how she invited her mother to Poland and provided her with notes containing useful phrases, which resulted in her mastering them after a short time. Another example may be admonishing compatriots about what linguistic behaviors should be avoided. As for Internet resources, a preliminary netnolinguistic survey revealed a large availability of materials on pronunciation, basic phrases, lexical differences and similarities, and, of course, vulgarisms and colloquialisms.

Linguistic biographies

Linguistic biography is the totality of practices and subjective experiences that make up the history of learning a foreign language by a given person. It is assumed that factors such as school experiences, individual learning, learning techniques, exercises performed, contact with cultural texts, text production, as well as memories related to the production and reception of speech influence the process of learning a foreign language by a given person. Biography understood in this way makes language learning an individual process and, in practice, cannot be fully unified. However, this does not exclude the possibility of con-structing models that allow categorizing and interpreting individual factors. Research on linguistic biographies is qualitative in nature. Data collection is carried out through field interviews in the interpretive paradigm or questionnaires sent via social media, mainly Facebook, Instagram, MS Teams, etc. (netnolinguistics). However, the interpretation of the collected data is carried out using discourse analysis tools: case study, examination of presuppositions, explicit and implicit content, metaphor analysis.

Understanding the learner's background is crucial for several reasons. First of all, it allows to retrospectively explain current language learning difficulties. A telling example may be microtraumas related to schooling, leading in adult life to inhibition of speech production, referred to in the literature as language anxiety. The interviews I conducted provide disturbingly numerous testimonies of incompetent behavior of teachers, who, through public ridicule and depreciation of learners' competences, contributed to the development of inhibition mechanisms related to anxiety.

Learning beliefs and subjective theories

The strictly psycholinguistic part of our project involves mapping and analyzing learners' subjective beliefs and theories about the language learning process, as well as the strategies, practices and procedures that these beliefs imply. The concept of beliefs about the language learning process is an important category that has been studied in applied linguistics for nearly forty years (Fazilatfar et al., 2014). The concept of learning beliefs was popularized in the 1980s by developmental psychologist Irving Sigel. The focus of this researcher's interest was representational competence: how people (children, students, parents, teachers, researchers) move from having a specific or basic understanding to understanding based on causal relationships, using symbols through which this understanding is represented. Learning beliefs can therefore be defined as "mental constructions of experience" (Sigel, 1985) that serve a functional purpose by guiding an agent's behavior. The belief systems that students accept as true help them adapt to new environments, define tasks, and understand what is expected of them (White 1999). In turn, in the Polish research tradition, in the context of teachers' beliefs, there is the concept of "subjective theories" originating from Anna Michońska-Stadnik (2013). While learning beliefs include practices and strategies that an individual belief system implies, subjective theories refer to the notion of language itself: the concepts concerning grammar, syntax and vocabulary, as well as their role in communication. Within the scope of our project, we consider these categories as complementary. In both cases it must be assumed that subjective beliefs and theories about learning necessarily shape not only the views and attitudes of students but also of teachers, and are reflected in the strategies, practices and explanatory regimes used in teaching (Riley, 1996;

Wenden 1999). It is therefore necessary to recognize the dynamics between these cognitive entities among learners in order to better understand their needs, formulate adequate and achievable goals, and adapt strategies consistent with the requirements we face.

Two research spaces: physical and virtual space

The transdisciplinary research on learning and teaching Polish as a foreign language among Ukrainians conducted as part of our project is carried out in two conventionally separated spaces: "physical" and "virtual". Aware of the increasing interpenetration of these spheres, we propose their pragmatic understanding in the following way:

- *Physical space or real world:* This space represents the tangible, physical environment where people meet face-to-face and engage in language learning and daily practice activities. It includes physical locations such as language schools, integration centers, cultural centers, workshops and social gatherings where Ukrainians meet to improve their language skills and cultural activities as part of extracurricular activities. Physical space also includes workplaces and spaces of traditional, personal interactions that play a significant role in language acquisition and cultural exchange: pubs, restaurants, sports and recreation centers.
- *Virtual or online space:* includes the digital sphere where language learners and the Polish-speaking community meet each other and engage in online interactions and learning activities. This space includes various online platforms and social media networks such as language learning apps, forums, social networking sites and educational websites. In this virtual environment, individuals have the opportunity to establish contacts, exchange information and learn Polish remotely, which makes it a valuable complement to their real-world language learning experiences.

Both spaces defined in this way become a field of field research carried out using adapted ethnographic and netnographic methods. Moreover, numerous methods developed by cultural anthropology are used in virtual space. In our case, they are: structured interview, survey, participant observation, non-participant observation, mental notes, etc. These methods fit into two complementary paradigms of fieldwork in cultural anthropology, which will be discussed below.

Two paradigms in field research: interpretive and processual

Interpretive paradigm

The main epistemological assumption of interpretive paradigm in anthropology is constructivism. The matter of the study is therefore meaning, the carrier of which is language, or more precisely, the respondents' statements. The role of the researcher is to interpret the statements of the Other, who becomes his partner and interlocutor (cited in: T. Buliński, 2014: 99). Therefore, in the case of our research project, the starting point of the proposed reflection are the statements of learners and teachers, and the role of the researcher is to interpret their experiences and opinions in the light of the problem posed.

The interpretive paradigm is usually understood as a key cognitive tool in the analysis of data collected through interviews and open questionnaires. A researcher who has field notes, interview transcripts, respondents' open answers or mental notes uses narrative analysis methods in the interpretation process. In this approach, the subject's statement (narrative) is examined as the only carrier of his or her beliefs and experiences available for viewing. Discourse analysis and thematic analysis may be auxiliary tools in data analysis, the specifics of which will be outlined later in the article.

An example of the use of the interpretive paradigm can be field and netnographic interviews (Messenger, Instagram) with Ukrainian speakers of Polish, in which we ask about their experiences of learning Polish in Poland and Ukraine, the strategies used, beliefs about learning and educational needs.

Processual paradigm

In the processual paradigm, the very object of study is the process itself. The events, practices and phenomena are observed in their change and evolution over time. The main epistemological assumption of this paradigm is perspectivism. Perspectivism is an epistemological model in the humanities that emphasizes subjectivity and the multiplicity of perspectives in understanding the world and human phenomena. It assumes that knowledge is not absolute, but rather depends on the observer's point of view, cultural context and individual experiences. In the perspectivist approach, the researcher also recognizes that his or her own background and beliefs influence his or her interpretation of phenomena. Perspectivism thus encourages the consideration of a wide range of points of view in order to obtain a more complete understanding of the complexity of social phenomena. By adopting perspectivism, the humanities seek to bridge the gap between objectivity and subjectivity and recognize the value of different perspectives in enriching our understanding of human experience.

Within the research lens understood in this way, the Other becomes an Accomplice, and the researcher becomes a tool for generating experiences. Here, too, experience is an important element of the study. The researcher not only records and interprets the respondents' statements, but also works to induce new experiences that will allow for a better understanding of the phenomenon under study. In this approach, the researcher and the researched jointly construct knowledge about the phenomenon under study.

Data collection: surveys, interviews and questionnaires, fieldnotes and headnotes

As part of the perspective model discussed above, it is necessary to propose several complementary methods of data collection consistent with the assumptions of the transdisciplinary approach. Given the diversity of migration scenarios, experiences, goals, needs and learning strategies, traditional methods of psycholinguistic and glottodidactic research are supplemented, as part of the triangulation of research methods, with techniques developed by social anthropology.

The first is a quantitative survey, the aim of which is to observe, on a representative research sample, the correlation between employee and social integration strategies, social capital and the forms of teaching and learning processes of the Polish language. Thematically divided questions concern, among others: the educational past of the respondents, their bilingualism, migration experiences, knowledge of the Polish language, preferred learning strategies, goals in personal and professional life connected to learning Polish, etc.

The second method of obtaining data is interviews, which are part of the qualitative research. They consist of semi-structured interviews between researchers and respondents, during which information is obtained about experiences and opinions on teaching Polish. Whenever possible, interviews take place during physical meetings with respondents – then the researcher records the answers in the questionnaire. However, if a physical meeting is not possible, respondents receive a form with open questions via social media. Data collected through interviews and questionnaires are analyzed within the interpretive paradigm discussed above. Both interviews and questionnaires allow for the collection of more detailed information about the experiences and needs of respondents. They can thus contribute to the confrontation of quantitative data with qualitative data (triangulation).

The third proposed method is the creation of field notes and mental notes (fieldnotes and headnotes). Fieldnotes are notes recorded by researchers during observations of educational situations and conversations and interviews. Headnotes, i. e. mental notes, are a record of notes after the observation process is completed. Headnotes contain the researcher's reflections on the observed behaviors of people teaching and learning in a given educational context. This method will allow collecting data on actual practices of teaching Polish among Ukrainian immigrants. It should be noted that both forms of records described above, being key anthropological tools, should not be alien to other practicing researchers of linguistic phenomena: individual observations and experiences of a teacher, a learner, a volunteer, and even a private person interacting with learners on a daily basis. Polish language, constitute valuable research material that can contribute to a deeper understanding of the studied phenomena. In both the interpretive and processual paradigms, the researcher's individual experience is a legitimate source of information that should not be ignored.

The data collection methods proposed above are complementary and constitute a valuable source of information on learning and teaching Polish as a foreign language among Ukrainian immigrants in Poland. Their use will allow for the collection of knowledge from various perspectives, enabling an in-depth examination of the problem thanks to the confrontation of quantitative data obtained through surveys with the results of qualitative research obtained through interviews and observations.

Observation: participant and non-participant

Field research among people from Ukraine learning and teaching Polish as a foreign language is conducted using two complementary forms of observation. The observations carried out as part of our project are not limited to physical space. As we will show below, observation techniques developed by cultural anthropology are also used in research conducted on the Internet.

The method of observation is one of the basic research tools of contemporary cultural anthropology, regardless of the adopted paradigm. Using field observation techniques, the researcher tries to understand the functioning of a given phenomenon in the natural environment and the impact that various social and cultural factors have on it. As part of the research on out-of-school Polish language learning among Ukrainians, participant observation, non-participant observation, and case studies are used.

In participant observation, which is part of the processual paradigm, the researcher immerses himself in the social environment under study, becoming an active participant in the practices and interactions of the group. The researcher can take on a specific role within the group, which allows him or her to gain an "insider's perspective" and a deeper understanding of the group's culture, behavior, and dynamics. Participant observation allows for obtaining detailed and insightful information about the reality under study, thanks to the fact that the researcher can directly experience its aspects and behaviors. This method is particularly useful in anthropological, sociological or psychological research, where the researcher wants to understand a culture, a social group or an individual in a way as close as possible to their everyday experience.

In participant observation, the researcher may use various techniques, such as conducting conversations, recording his or her experiences and impressions, participating in events, and analyzing the language and culture used in the researched environment. An example of the use of such research in netnography is participation in groups on social media, where people learning Polish gather to exchange knowledge and experiences. Participant observation in such an environment allows for interaction with people learning Polish by providing them with support and guidance. By analyzing the most common queries, problems, as well as strategies for solving them, we gain insight into the real needs of learners.

An example of the use of participant observation as part of our project is the above-mentioned study by Zbigniew Szmyt in the process paradigm. Becoming a participant in a massage course at a school for migrants allowed the researcher to integrate with the research subjects and participate in their experiences. This method can sometimes be difficult in practice because it requires a lot of time and commitment, and may also raise ethical problems, such as the need to maintain confidentiality or a conflict of interest between the role of participant and researcher. Therefore, it is complemented by a second type of observation: non-participant observation.

Unlike participant observation, non-participant observation involves the researcher observing subjects without directly engaging or participating in their activities. Therefore, this is a study that fits into the interpretative paradigm. The researcher maintains a more detached posture, often using techniques such as discreet observation from a distance. This method allows for more objective data collection because subjects may behave more naturally when they are unaware that they are being observed. This method, however, does not provide the insight into the inner functioning of the group that participant observation offers, therefore both methods should complement each other.

Netnolinguistics

Netnolinguistics is an innovative research concept proposed as part of the described research project. Drawing on the Konzinets' concept of *netnography* (Kozinets 2020), we understand netnolinguistics as an area of transdisciplinary research activities, focusing on the study of linguistic phenomena in the context of social interactions, ethnological conditions and practices in the online environment. Netnolinguistics combines elements of linguistics, ethnography and internet studies to explore the complex connections between language, culture, and technology in online communication. Its aim is to discover the sociolinguistic patterns, pragma linguistic communication practices and dynamic psycholinguistic processes that emerge in online spaces, shedding light on the interplay of online culture, peer interaction, identity construction and language use (Paradowski, Jarynowski, Czopek Jelińska 2021). Netnolinguistics also emphasizes the role of non-human agents in linguistic processes, including learning and teaching foreign languages. The elements of actor-network theory (Latour 2005) and the posthumanist perspective (Bruun 2022; Whitehead, Wesch 2012) are also used as part of the research on the interaction between an online learner and non-human agents, such as devices, applications, social media platforms etc. The notion of assemblage coined by Deleuze and Guattari (Deleuze, Guattari 1987) enables to conceptualize the specific relation between human and non-human agents within the frame of the learning situation: it emphasizes not only the teacher-learner interaction but also the dynamics between the network of non-human elements of the process (computer or mobile phone) and virtual structures like application, interface, chat, etc. By analyzing interactions and discursive strategies used in digital contexts, netnolinguistics aims at deepening the understanding of the multifaceted relationship between language, society, and technology in the digital age.

In the context of the research on extracurricular PFL learning among Ukrainians, the main objective is to examine the *technology mediated language learning* (Friedman, George 2022). Netnolinguistic research as part of our project focuses primarily on the analysis of PFL teaching materials present in the virtual environment, in media such as YouTube, Instagram or TikTok. Furthermore, qualitative interviews have been led with creators of educational content in order to recognize their learning biographies and subjective theories of language acquisition. The key questions posed in such research concern the preferred forms of presentation of linguistic content, the heuristics used and the pragmatic selection of content in relation to needs and their perceived usefulness.

The basic methodological practices of netnolinguistics are interviews using various communication platforms: Messenger, Instagram, TikTok, etc. At the same time, it is important to observe practices, interactions and methods of communication between users in order to better understand the demographic and identity aspects of learning Polish: biographical contexts, needs and motivations. The main tool used in the study of netnolinguistic content is discourse analysis, which we discuss below.

Discourse analysis

Within the scope of our project, discourse analysis is understood as a research approach that focuses on examining linguistic and non-linguistic elements of discourse (i. e. statements, conversations, texts that create a coherent set) in order to understand and interpret the meanings contained in them. Both written texts, such as essays, posts and comments, as well as recorded oral speech and short audiovisual materials shared by social media users constitute potential material for discourse analysis.

This method is in particular valuable in extracting the subjective content and beliefs that shape the speakers' statements and practices in learning. The study of individual narratives allows to "translate" subjective testimonies into the language of contemporary psycholinguistic and glottodidactic theories. An example of such an explanation may be inferring from learners' practices and statements about their subjective theory of language and its acquisition. The analysis of interviews conducted among Ukrainians who do not have a philological background and work, for example, in the catering industry, suggests an instrumental concept of language oriented towards practical communication (Krzyżosiak 2024). This concept implies specific adaptive practices characterized by selective learning of vocabulary related to the immediate environment and simplified inflectional and syntactic models necessary in simple, everyday professional communication. It is important to note that linguistic adaptation understood in this way turns out to be largely functional. In turn, the analysis of the experiences of learners in interaction with native speakers of Polish, collected in the interview, suggests that in the intercultural context the perception of language norms and errors by Polish women and men interacting with Ukrainians changes. Indeed, the respondents observed high tolerance and understanding of Polish interlocutors for the mistakes they made. Therefore, it can be argued that the friendliness of native speakers contributes to reducing the share of negative emotions in the communication process, creating conditions conducive to practicing newly acquired competences.

Summary

The proposed transdisciplinary model in the study mapping out-of-school practices of learning and teaching Polish among Ukrainians is adapted to the multidimensional complexity of the problem addressed. The key aspect of the outlined approach is the dynamic complementation of the research approaches and practices used. This allows researchers to exceed the limitations of individual methods used separately. This is how a specific dialectic of complementary methods and concepts is formed:

Object of study	Migrant knowledge	Linguistic biographies, learning beliefs, subjective theories
Research space	Real (physical)	Virtual
Field research framework	Processual (participant observation)	Interpretive (non-participant observation)
Virtual research framework	Netnography	Netnolinguistics
Data collection	Surveys (quantitative)	Interviews, observation, (qualitative)
Data analysis	Analysis of practices, interactions and identity construction (anthropology)	Discourse analysis (linguistics)

1. In conceptualizing problems and defining research goals, the anthropological concept of migrant knowledge is complemented by linguistic concepts of linguistic biography and subjective beliefs and theories about learning.
2. Research activities taking place in real (physical) space are complemented by research in virtual space.
3. In field research, the physical and logistical limitations of participant observation in the processual paradigm are complemented by distanced, non-participant observation in the interpretative paradigm.
4. In the virtual sphere, the framework of netnographic research developed to gather ethnographic data among users of digital platforms is completed by netnolinguistics tailored to observe and analyze linguistic data in social contexts.
5. General quantitative information obtained through surveys is supplemented by interviews providing qualitative data.
6. In the interpretation of the acquired data, linguistic methods, such as discourse analysis and thematic analysis, complement traditional anthropological methods, such as the analysis of practices, interactions and identity construction.

It is important to emphasize that the proposed methodological model is not a permanent and closed entity. It should rather be viewed as a transdisciplinary "toolbox" that can be supplemented with new concepts and research solutions, depending on the needs of the research being conducted. For this reason, we hope that the methodological solutions we presented will be successfully adapted and used in different fields of studies in applied linguistics.

Bibliography

Ahearn Laura N. (2017) Living Language – An Introduction to Linguistic Anthropology. Wiley Blackwell, Oxford.

Buliński T. (2014) Ruchoma wiedza terenowa. Perspektywa antropologii procesualnej. Zeszyty Etnologii Wrocławskiej nr 2014/2(21), ISSN 1642-0977.

Chava Frankfort-Nachmias, David Nachmias (2001) Metody badawcze w naukach społecznych. Zysk i S-ka, Poznań. S. 297.

Deleuze G., Guattari F. (1987) A Thousand Plateaus: Capitalism and Schizophrenia. University of Minnesota Press.

Fazilatfar (et al.) (2014) Learners' Belief Changes about Language Learning. International Journal of English Language Education.

Friedman R., George A. (eds.) (2022) Online Language Teaching in Diverse Contexts. Cambridge Scholars Publishing, Newcastle.

Gębal P.E. (red.) (2018) Edukacja wobec migracji: konteksty glottodydaktyczne i pedagogiczne. Księgarnia Akademicka, Kraków.

Kita, M. (2012) Razem: konsiliencja, interdyscyplinarność, transdyscyplinarność. In: M. Kita, M. Ślawska (eds.) "Transdyscyplinarność badań nad komunikacją medialną. T. 1, Stan wiedzy i postulaty badawcze". Wydawnictwo Uniwersytetu Śląskiego, Katowice.

Kozinets R. (2020) Netnography: The Essential Guide to Qualitative Social Media Research. Sage Publications Ltd, London.

Latour B. (2005) Reassembling the Social: An Introduction to Actor-Network-Theory. Oxford UP, Oxford.

Levchuk P. (2020) Trójjęzyczność ukraińsko-rosyjsko-polska w Ukraińców niepolskiego pochodzenia. Księgarnia Akademicka, Kraków.

Michońska-Stadnik A. (2013) Teoretyczne i praktyczne podstawy weryfikacji wybranych teorii subiektywnych w kształceniu nauczycieli języków obcych. Wydawnictwo Uniwersytetu Wrocławskiego, Wrocław.

Nawracka M. J. (2020) Nauczanie języka polskiego jako obcego w perspektywie refleksyjnej i kulturowej. Księgarnia Akademicka, Kraków.

Pamuła-Behrens M., Hennel-Brzozowska A. (eds.) (2019) Migration and Education. To Understand Relations between Migration and Education – Challenges for Research and Practice. Oficyna Wydawnicza Impuls, Kraków.

Paltridge B. (2020) "Multi-perspective research" in: J. McKinley, H. Rose (eds.) The Routledge Handbook of Research Methods in Applied Linguistics. Routledge, New York.

Paradowski M., Jarynowski A., Czopek K., Jelińska, (2021) "Peer interactions and second language learning: The contributions of Social Network Analysis in Study Abroad vs At-Home environments". In: Mitchell, Rosamond & Henry Tyne (eds.), Language, Mobility and Study Abroad in the Contemporary European Context, Routledge, Oxon, pp. 99–116.

Paradowski M., Jarynowski A., Jelińska M., Czopek K. (2021) Out-of-class peer inter-actions matter for second language acquisition during short-term overseas sojourns. The contributions of Social Network Analysis, Language Teaching. Surveys and Studies, Volume 54, Issue 1, pp. 139–143.

Rajaram Prem Kumar (2022) Refugee and migrant knowledge as historical narratives. Routledge, University of Helsinki. DOI: 10.4324/9781003092421-4 Refugees and Knowledge Production.

Renninger, K. A. (2007) Obituary: Irving E. (Irv) Sigel (1921–2006). American Psychologist, 62(4), 321. https://doi.org/10.1037/0003-066X.62.4.321.

Sułkowski Ł., Przytuła S., Migdał M.A. (2020) Skilled Ukrainian migrants in the Polish emerging economy: implications for knowledge management. European J. International Management, Vol. 14, No. 5.

Sztabiński P. et al. (2005) Fieldwork jest sztuką – jak dobrać respondenta, skłonić go do udziału w wywiadzie, rzetelnie i sprawnie zrealizować badanie. Wydawnictwo Instytutu Filozofii i Socjologii PAN, Warszawa.

Thoma N. (2022) Biographical perspectives on language ideologies in teacher education. Language and Education, Volume 36, issue 5.

White C. (2008) Beliefs and good language learners. Cambridge University Press, Cambridge.

Whitehead N., Wesch M. (2012) Human No More: Digital Subjectivities, Unhuman Subjects, and the End of Anthropology. University Press of Colorado, Denver.

Williams A. (2007) Listen to me, learn with me: International migration and knowledge. British Journal of Industrial Relations, 45(2), pp. 361–382.

Part Two.
Migrant tuition and Intercomprehension

Jacopo Saturno (Università di Bergamo)

Intercomprehension, transfer and L2 Polish

Abstract

The present paper suggests that intercomprehension, one of the pillars of the so-called "plural approaches" commonly advocated for the development of pluri- and multilingualism, may play a particularly significant role in the Polish context. More specifically, it is argued that despite the traditional focus on receptive skills, this approach may nonetheless greatly favour the acquisition of L2 Polish in two potentially large groups of learners, i.e. speakers of Slavic languages as L1, on the one hand, and learners of other Slavic languages as L2, on the other hand. In both cases, learners could capitalise on their existing knowledge of Slavic languages closely related to the target language, thus devoting significantly fewer resources to the learning of those grammatical categories (e.g. nominal case, verbal aspect) that typically constitute notable obstacles for beginner learners, and focussing instead on the points in which the languages in contact diverge.

Introduction: intercomprehension

IC refers to a relationship between languages in which speakers of different but related languages can partially understand each other without explicit knowledge of the language of the interlocutor. From a narrow perspective, IC may be defined as "a relationship between languages in which speakers of different but related languages can readily understand each other without intentional study or extraordinary effort" (European Commission 2012). From a broader perspective, it can be seen as a general ability to "understand languages without speaking them" (Blanche-Benveniste & Valli, 1997). The partial comprehensibility of the target language is made possible by substantial positive transfer – in terms of grammar and vocabulary – from another language known to the reader or listener, traditionally labelled *bridge language*.

IC has been long advocated as a tool to satisfy the need for international communication while preserving linguistic and cultural diversity (Candelier et al. 2007; Council of Europe 2019); as such, it is often portrayed as a valid alternative to the diffusion of English as a Lingua Franca (ELF), which in turn is accompanied by the risk of "linguistic imperialism" (Philipson 1992). Eco (1995: 351) in particular argues the following:

> "Polyglot Europe will not be a continent where individuals converse fluently in all the other languages; in the best of cases, it could be a continent where differences of language are no longer barriers to communication, where people can meet each other and speak together, each in his or her tongue, understanding, as best they can, the speech of others. In this way, even those who never learn to speak another language fluently could still participate in its particular genius, catching a glimpse of the particular cultural universe that every individual expresses each time he or she speaks the language of his or her ancestors and his or her own tradition".

It is evident that the focus here is on the development of receptive, rather than productive skills[1]. Nevertheless, it will be argued here that the contingencies that make intercomprehension possible are also fertile ground for the acquisition of the unknown language to happen, a goal that is usually not contemplated by research on the subject. Indeed, intercomprehensibility seems to imply a certain familiarity of the reader or listener not only with the lexicon of the unknown language, but also its grammar. The advantage of already knowing words that are similar (though not necessarily identical: see 1.2.1) to their counterpart in the unknown language is quite evident; concerning grammar, although it has been long argued that the learners' real priority in second language acquisition is in fact the lexicon (cf. VanPatten's (2015) "primacy of meaning" principle), partial familiarity with the structure of the unknown language may positively affect the rate and ease of its acquisition. Since no new cognitive categories need developing, learners with knowledge of related languages may feel more at ease with a variety of morphosyntactic cues to grammatical meaning (e. g. case marking as a cue to syntactic function), while exclusive reliance on the L1 system might prompt them to focus on the cues that are most reliable in the L1, but not necessarily in the target language. To exemplify, it has been shown that compared to speakers of L1s with complex verbal morphology, such as Russian, Spanish, and Romanian, speakers of L1s with poorer verbal morphology, such as Chinese and English, tend to rely more on L2 adverbs than L2 verbal morphology (Ellis & Sagarra 2011; Sagarra & Ellis 2013). Altogether, therefore, it seems that the (theoretical) possibility of intercomprehension could also be interpreted more broadly in terms of cross-linguistic influence (Jarvis & Pavlenko 2007; Alonso Alonso 2016), i. e. as a particular contingency facilitating language learning acquisition.

---

1 Another popular strand in research on "classic" intercomprehension concerns the positive impact of intercomprehension on the development of metalinguistic and "strategic" skills (Ustaszewski 2014; Bonvino et al. 2018; Fiorenza 2019).

These considerations seem to fit the case of L2 Polish particularly well. While Polish did not use to be a commonly taught foreign or second language (with the partial exception of the Polish diaspora and the areas inhabited by Polish minorities, see Levchuk & Stapor 2022), very recent changes of political, social and economic nature have remarkably changed this picture. Indeed, Poland has recently attracted large numbers of speakers of Slavic languages, first as economic migrants, subsequently as refugees fleeing the conflict in Ukraine. At the same time, non-Slavic speakers of L2 Russian (which is both a commonly taught foreign language and a close relative of Polish) may now feel inclined to learn Polish in connection with Poland's growing importance on the labour market and the political arena. This paper aims to argue that intercomprehension may set the foundation of language teaching approaches and materials aiming to teach L2 Polish quickly and effectively to speakers of closely related Slavic languages, a goal that seems justified by the numerous similarities between these codes.

Intercomprehension as a language teaching tool

The idea to use intercomprehension as a language teaching tool is not new. Some very successful manuals, such as Eurom4 (Blanche-Benveniste 1997) and Eurom5 (Bonvino et al. 2011) emphasize the potential of this approach to develop strategic and metalinguistic skills; others, like EuroComRom (Klein & Stegmann 2000) and EuroComGerm (Hufeisen & Marx 2007), while not explicitly mentioning a language learning goal, aim to provide the reader with a set of linguistic information deemed useful to better decode a text in an unknown, but partially intelligible language. Other publications explicitly aim to develop language skills (primarily receptive) through quick, effective language courses designed for learners with knowledge of languages related to the object of learning, like the Czech course by Townsend and Komar (2000) and the Bulgarian course by Gribble (2013), both for speakers of Russian. The rationale of these approaches is quite similar: the decoding of transparent linguistic items and features is left to the user's intuition, which makes it possible to allocate greater resources to the analysis of cross-linguistic differences or the development of productive skills.

At the same time, the intercomprehension approach moves away from traditional language instruction in a variety of ways. To start, it explicitly envisages the presence of multiple languages during classes. This is consistent with the recommendation of the CEFR, starting at least from its 2001 edition: "the aim of language education […] is no longer seen to achieve 'mastery' of one or two, or even three languages, each taken in isolation, with the 'ideal native speaker' as the ultimate model, […] but to develop a linguistic repertoire, in which all linguistic abilities have a place (CEF, 2001, p. 5)". Nevertheless, the idea that considering more than one related languages at the same time may lead to interference is still widespread, to the extent that even in an IC context, the detrimental effects attributable to negative transfer (e.g. "false friends", the selection of incorrect inflectional endings etc.) is sometimes considered (especially by language teachers) to outweigh the advantages of positive influence (Saturno 2023b).

Secondly, the idea of a progression in the complexity of the teaching material does not necessarily reflect the actual process of approaching a new target language through intercomprehension. This is because adult learners have native mastery of at least one language and can therefore draw from any layers of it in order to make inferences as to the target language (Rast 2010), regardless of the frequency or complexity of the linguistic item considered. Thus, sophisticated technical terms or words referring to uncommon *realia* may be perfectly transparent and thus create no difficulty. This applies to both internationalisms, e.g. Pol. *radioteleskop* 'radio telescope' (virtually identical to its Russian counterpart), and words belonging to a given sub-group of languages, e.g. Pol. *śmietana*, Rus. *smetana* 'sour cream'. It follows that from the very beginning, the learner may approach material "which was not written for a textbook, but which is intended for native speakers of the language and is interesting for the message conveyed, and not just because of the grammatical material presented" (Gribble 2013: 12).

Intercomprehension in practice: receptive and productive skills

It should be noted, however, that research on so far has mainly focused on the development of receptive skills, while productive skills have been somewhat neglected. This may be thought to originate from two circumstances: first, intercomprehension in a narrow sense envisages a communicative situation in which all interlocutors speak their own language, so that the development of productive skills in a foreign language is not *stricto sensu* required[2]. In that scenario, the research on *interproduction* (Balboni 2007; Ollivier 2017; Capucho 2018) may prove particularly useful for the training of those speakers of Polish who are more likely to provide humanitarian assistance, with the aim to minimize the possibilities of communication failures due to this interaction mode.

Second, while reception involves the recognition of a *given* element, which only needs interpreting, speaking involves the *production* of a form that needs to

---

2 Indeed, this claim has attracted the critique that intercomprehension may in fact instantiate "another manifestation of a monolingual ideology in the sense that accepting to understand another language could be the condition for refusing to speak it actively" (Lüdi et al. 2010: 75).

be recognizable by the interlocutor. Based on the intuitive analysis of the input they are exposed to, learners may adopt strategies aimed to maximize the probability that their creative produced forms match the intended target and or are at least recognizable; for instance, learners of L2 Polish were reported to quickly identify the morpheme -*k*- as a frequent word formation element and use it in their own output when asked to produce – rather, to guess – the unknown word describing a difficult profession, e. g. [vidʒilka] 'policewoman' from It. *vigile* 'traffic ward' (Saturno 2020). Similarly, Spanish learners of L2 French were shown to regularly omit the final sound cluster of Spanish words in order to obtain what they hypothesized to be its French cognate, as in [pro'blɛm] for French /pʀo'blɛm/, cf. Spanish /pro'blemas/ 'problems'; however, there are cases in which such strategies utterly fail, e. g. [pwed] for French /pøv/ '(they) can', cf. Spanish /'pweden/ (Giacobbe & Cammarota 1986: 253). Thus, as far as production is concerned, there is always a risk of communication failure when target language items are produced (or, rather, guessed) without exact knowledge of their phonological representation (unlike the prototypical case in "traditional" SLA: the learner either knows or does not know that target item). The problem of the learner's conformity to the norm of the target language becomes particularly urgent in the case of schoolchildren and knowledge workers, who are required to express themselves in a manner that is not only communicatively effective, but also appropriate in light of social conventions.

Two groups of learners

In the case of L2 Polish, what has been argued so far seems to apply to two radically different groups of potential learners, i. e. East Slavic economic migrants and refugees, on the other hand, and students of Slavic languages as foreign languages, on the other hand. Despite their obvious and conspicuous discrepancies, these groups also share a common trait that in principle makes intercomprehension a valid language teaching approach, i. e. the existing knowledge of another Slavic language.

Native speakers of East Slavic languages are by far the most numerous group, since in recent times Poland has welcomed a significant population of citizens of Ukraine, first in connection with its economic growth, later on as a consequence of the humanitarian crisis caused by the conflict in Ukraine (Główny Urząd Statystyczny 2020; Unia Metropolii Polskich 2022). From a linguistic point of view, Ukrainian refugees are speakers of closely related Slavic languages, among which Russian, Ukrainian, and the continuum of mixed varieties collectively known as *suržyk* (Hentschel et al. 2014). Independently of their long-term plans – some may wish to return to their homes as soon as possible, while other may prefer to remain in Poland for a longer time –, refugees and economic migrants alike obviously need to integrate linguistically – at least to some extent – into Polish society. Clearly, this goal is all the more urgent for foreign children attending Polish schools.

Students of Slavic languages, on the other, typically have varying proficiency in L2 Russian, while other Slavic languages (including Polish) are not quite as commonly taught, at least in the Western higher education system. This is still true despite the steep decrease in popularity experienced by L2 Russian following the hostilities in Ukraine and the ensuing economic sanctions, which effectively limited the possibilities to trade with Russian and, consequently, the need for language experts in this area. On the other hand, it is quite remarkable that Polish is not a particularly commonly taught foreign language, in spite of its being the largest Slavic EU language in terms of speaker (and the second largest Slavic language worldwide, following Russian); Polish is also the language of a country that has experienced a rapid and significant economic growth in the last decades and is not increasingly active on the international scene, a role that is probably destined to grow with the reconstruction of Ukraine.

Although West and East Slavic languages constitute two separate sub-groups within the group of Slavic languages, they are nonetheless closely related in terms of grammar and vocabulary (Heeringa et al. 2023), which in principle constitutes fertile ground for intercomprehension to occur. Clearly, L1 speakers of East Slavic varieties and students of L2 Russian may have very different linguistic profiles, especially as far as broadly understood lexical competence is concerned (Zareva 2012): as a rule, native speakers' access to the lexicon is both broader (i. e. they know a greater number of lexical elements) and more profound (i. e. they have better mastery of the lexical items properties, including polysemy, collocations etc.). On the other hand, the educated foreign language learner may also enjoy some advantages, such as a broader language repertoire as well as greater metalinguistic awareness. The latter in particular can be fruitfully exploited to target aspects of language that are particularly problematic for beginner learners, such as phonology (Marx & Mehlhorn 2010) or, in the case of Slavic languages, inflectional morphology (Saturno 2022) and verbal aspect (Noseda & Saturno 2024).

Conclusion

Research on intercomprehension has gone a long way in the past few decades; however, it may well gain new inspiration from the challenges dictated by the present international contingencies. The case of present-day Poland is particularly instructive in this respect. A language that is likely to significantly increase its social and economic importance, Polish is markedly close to East Slavic languages; these in turn are the native languages of numerous economic migrants and refugees that in recent years have entered Poland, on the hand, and (with respect to Russian) a commonly taught foreign language. The partial intercomprehensibility of Polish through other Slavic languages – or, more neutrally, its similarity to them – to may enable speakers of Slavic to approach Polish more quickly and effortlessly than is usually the case (Polish often suffering from the stereotype of being "one of the most difficult languages to learn"; Saturno 2023a). A particularly pressing objective in this respect seems to be the development of large-scale, quick, and effective language courses for speakers of other Slavic languages, designed in light of the similarities between their native language(s) and the target language, and aiming to develop not only receptive, but also productive skills.

Bibliography

Alonso Alonso, Rosa (ed.). 2016. *Crosslinguistic influence in second language acquisition* (Second Language Acquisition 95). Bristol ; Buffalo: Multilingual Matters.

Balboni, Paolo. 2007. Dall'intercomprensione all'intercomunicazione romanza. In Capucho, Filomena & Martins, Adriana & Degache, Christian & Tost, Manuel (eds.), *Diálogos em intercompreensão*, 447–459. Lisboa: Universidade Catolica Ed.

Blanche-Benveniste, Claire (ed.). 1997. *EuRom 4: metodo di insegnamento simultaneo della lingue romanze*. Firenze: La nuova Italia.

Bonvino, Elisabetta & Caddéo, Sandrine & Serra, Eulalia & Pippa, Salvador (eds.). 2011. *EuRom5: leggere e capire 5 lingue romanze*. Milano: Hoepli.

Bonvino, Elisabetta & Fiorenza, Elisa & Cortés Velásquez, Diego. 2018. Observing Strategies in Intercomprehension Reading. Some Clues for Assessment in Plurilingual Settings. *Frontiers in Communication* 3. 29. (doi:10.3389/fcomm.2018.00029)

Candelier, Michel & Camilleri-Grima, Antoinette & Castellotti, Véronique & de Pietro, Jean-François & Lörincz, Ildikó & Meissner, Meißner, Franz-Joseph & Schröder-Sura, Anna & Noguerol, Artur. 2007. *CARAP – Cadre de référence pour les approches plurielles des langues et des cultures*. Graz: Council of Europe.

Capucho, Filomena. 2018. Plurilingual interactions – the role of interproduction strategies. In Hepp, Marianne & Nied Curcio, Martina (eds.), *Educazione plurilingue: ricerca, didattica e politiche linguistiche*, 157–166. Roma: Istituto Italiano di Studi Germanici.

Council of Europe. 2019. Council Recommendation of 22 May 2019 on a comprehensive approach to the teaching and learning of languages. *Official Journal of the European Union*.

Eco, Umberto. 1995. *The search for the perfect language*. Oxford: Wiley-Blackwell.

Ellis, Nick C. & Sagarra, Nuria. 2011. Learned attention in adult language acquisition: a Replication and Generalization Study and Meta-Analysis. *Studies in Second Language Acquisition* 33(04). 589–624. (doi:https://doi.org/10.1017/S0272263111000325)

European Commission. 2012. Translation and Multilingualism: Intercomprehension. Luxemburg: Publications Office of the European Union.

Fiorenza, Elisa. 2019. Investigating the role of metalinguistic awareness in foreign language acquisition in an Intercomprehension-based setting: An exploratory study. *Rivista di psicolinguistica applicata* (XIX). (https://doi.org/10.19272/201907702007)

Giacobbe, Jorge & Cammarota, Marie-Ange. 1986. Un Modello del Rapporto L1/L2 nella Costruzione del Lessico. In Giacalone Ramat, Anna (ed.), *L'apprendimento Spontaneo di una Seconda Lingua*, 245–264. Bologna: Il Mulino.

Główny Urząd Statystyczny. 2020. Populacja cudzoziemców w Polsce w czasie COVID-19. (https://stat.gov.pl/statystyki-eksperymentalne/kapital-ludzki/populacja-cudzoziemco w-w-polsce-w-czasie-covid-19,12,1.html)

Gribble, Charles. 2013. *Reading Bulgarian through Russian*. Bloomington: Slavica.

Heeringa, Wilbert & Gooskens, Charlotte & Van Heuven, Vincent J. 2023. Comparing Germanic, Romance and Slavic: Relationships among linguistic distances. *Lingua* 287. 103512. (doi:10.1016/j.lingua.2023.103512)

Hentschel, Gerd & Taranenko, Oleksandr & Zaprudski, Siarhej. 2014. *Trasjanka und Suržyk – gemischte weißrussisch-russische und ukrainisch-russische Rede*. Peter Lang. (doi:10.3726/978-3-653-05057-8)

Hufeisen, Britta & Marx, Nicole (eds.). 2007. *EuroComGerm – die sieben Siebe: germanische Sprachen lesen lernen* (Reihe EuroComGerm). Aachen: Shaker.

Jarvis, Scott & Pavlenko, Aneta. 2007. *Crosslinguistic Influence in Language and Cognition*. London: Routledge.

Klein, Horst G. & Stegmann, Tilbert Dídac. 2000. *EuroComRom – die sieben Siebe: romanische Sprachen sofort lesen können; [français, català, español, italiano, português, română]* (Editiones EuroCom 1). Aachen: Shaker.

Levchuk, Pavlo & Stapor, M. E. 2022. Nauczanie języka polskiego jako obcego i odziedziczonego na ukrainie i w norwegii. zarys problematyki. *Науковий вісник ДДПУ імені Івана Франка. Серія: Філологічні науки (мовознавство)* (17). 71–77. (doi:10.24919/ 2663-6042.17.2022.11)

Lüdi, Georges & Höchle, Katharina & Yanaprasart, Patchareerat. 2010. Patterns of language use in polyglossic urban areas and multilingual regions and institutions: a Swiss case study. *International Journal of the Sociology of Language* 2010(205). 55–78. (doi: 10.1515/ijsl.2010.039)

Marx, Nicole & Mehlhorn, Grit. 2010. Pushing the Positive: Encouraging Phonological Transfer from L2 to L3. *International Journal of Multilingualism* 7(1). 4–18. (doi:https:// doi.org/10.1080/14790710902972271)

Noseda, Valentina & Saturno, Jacopo. 2024. Metalinguistic transfer in Slavic intercomprehension: the case of verbal aspect. EuroSLA 33, Université de Montpellier.

Ollivier, Christian. 2017. L'interproduction: entre foreigner talk et spécificité en intercompréhension. In Degache, Christian & Garbarino, Sandra (eds.), *Itinéraires pédagogiques de l'alternance des langues*, 337–352. UGA Éditions. (doi:10.4000/books.ugaeditions.2097)

Philipson, Robert. 1992. *Linguistic imperialism*. Oxford: Oxford University Press.

Rast, Rebekah. 2010. The use of prior linguistic knowledge in the early stages of L3 acquisition. *International Review of Applied Linguistics in Language Teaching* 48(2/3). 159–183. (doi:DOI 10.1515/iral.2010.008)

Sagarra, Nuria & Ellis, Nick. 2013. From Seeing Adverbs to Seeing Verbal Morphology. *Studies in Second Language Acquisition* 35(02). 261–290. (doi:https://doi.org/10.1017/S0272263112000885)

Saturno, Jacopo. 2020. Word formation in the earliest stages of L2 Polish: The use of derivational morphology in reference to human entities. *Language, Interaction and Acquisition* 11(2). 232–267. (doi:10.1075/lia.19012.sat)

Saturno, Jacopo. 2022. Production of inflectional morphology in intercomprehension-based language teaching: the case of Slavic languages. *International Journal of Multilingualism* 19(3). 383–401. (doi:10.1080/14790718.2020.1730379)

Saturno, Jacopo. 2023a. Stereotypy JPjO wśród różnych grup uczących się. Nauczanie języka polskiego jako obcego wobec wyzwań współczesnego świata, Uniwersytet Szczeciński.

Saturno, Jacopo. 2023b. Bliskość pomiędzy językami słowiańskimi a integracja uchodźców z Ukrainy w Polsce. *Poznańskie Studia Polonistyczne. Seria Językoznawcza* 30(1). 153–176. (doi:https://doi.org/10.14746/pspsj.2023.30.1.9)

Townsend, Charles E & Komar, Eric S. 2000. *Czech through Russian*. Bloomington: Slavica.

Unia Metropolii Polskich. 2022. Miejska gościnność: wielki wzrost, wyzwania i szanse. Raport o uchodźcach z Ukrainy w największych polskich miastach. Centrum Analiz i Badań, Unia Metropolii Polskich im. Pawła Adamowicza.

Ustaszewski, Michael. 2014. *Towards a methodology for intercomprehension-based language instruction in translator training*. University of Innsbruck. (Ph.D. dissertation.)

VanPatten, Bill. 2015. Foundations of processing instruction. *International Review of Applied Linguistics in Language Teaching* 53(2). 91–109. (doi:10.1515/iral-2015-0005)

Zareva, Alla. 2012. Partial word knowledge: Frontier words in the L2 mental lexicon. *International Review of Applied Linguistics in Language Teaching* 50(4). 277–301. (doi:10.1515/iral-2012-0011)

Aneta Lewińska (University of Gdańsk)

A case study – The work of a Polish teacher on developing the vocabulary of a student with a migration experience in the perspective of intercomprehension

Abstract

Intercomprehension allows students and teachers of multilingual classrooms to understand each other in everyday school communication, but the work of a Polish language teacher teaching Polish in a multilingual classroom is not enough. Knowledge and linguistic awareness are needed, as well as adequate didactic competence. Planning such difficult didactic work requires prior diagnosis and recognition of the difficulties faced by the student and the teacher. An element of such diagnosis is the written work of students. For Polish teachers who do not know Russian, they generate many difficulties, especially at the level of word comprehension. Investigating the strategies of dealing with incomprehensible words by Polish and Polish studies students allows us to see the problems of teaching vocabulary of the second language and to propose didactic solutions.

In a Polish school today, there sit[1] next to each other: Polish children, children of other nationalities (most often from Ukraine and Belarus) with the experience of labor migration, sometimes residing in Poland for several years, and Ukrainian children with the experience of refugeeism.

In one classroom, there are students for whom Polish is their native and first language, and students for whom Polish is a foreign language (though related to their native language) and is slowly becoming a second language, and may in the future become their functional first language.

In this linguistically and culturally diverse classroom, the teacher organises and conducts many hours of Polish lessons each week. Pursuing the primary goal inscribed in the basic Curriculum for General Education for Elementary Schools, he/she aims for all students to master "the ability to communicate in the native

---

1 According data from February 2024, there are 277.3 thousand Ukrainian children and youth in Polish schools and nurseries, including 180.1, thousand who came from Ukraine to Poland after the Russian aggression against their country, according to data from the Ministry of Education https://www.gazetaprawna.pl/wiadomosci/kraj/artykuly/9440304,men-w-systemie -edukacji-mamy-ponad-180-tys-dzieci-i-mlodziezy-z-ukra.html.

language and in a foreign language, both in speech and in writing"[2]. At the same time, for many of its students, Polish is not a native language, but a foreign language. The 2017 provision from the ordinance of Minister of National Education takes on a different meaning in 2023 than that projected by the creators of this document. The Polish language teacher becomes simultaneously a teacher of Polish – the native language and Polish language as a foreign language, which requires new competencies, especially in the field of language knowledge and methods of teaching the second and subsequent languages.

One of the biggest challenges facing the student is mastering the written variety of the second language[3], and before the teacher such a construction of the curriculum in a multilingual classroom that this skill is developed both in students for whom Polish is the first (native) language and those for whom it is the second or third language. Planning such difficult didactic work requires prior diagnosis and recognition of the difficulties faced by the student and the teacher.

The Faculty of Philology at the University of Gdansk has been implementing the project[4] *Communication Barriers of Migrants in the Polish-Speaking Environment since June 2021. The situation of Slavic and non-Slavic speakers living in the Pomeranian region.* An important part of this project is the analysis of the difficulties faced by children with migrant experience starting or continuing their education in Polish educational institutions, and in whose case the communication barrier is often responsible for school failure. Research on this problem is served, among other things, by the "FoKo" Polish Language Pupil Corpus, created by a team of linguists from the University of Gdansk, collecting, among other things, written works of children (who are non-native speakers of Polish) studying in primary and secondary schools from the Pomeranian Voivodeship.

The corpus is constantly being expanded and successively developed by linguists from the Institute of Polish Philology, the Institute of Speech Therapy and the Institute of Russian and Eastern Studies at the University of Gdansk. It contains several hundred student essays written on one selected from three topics: 1) *My happiest day in life*; 2) *My greatest hero*; 3) *The school of the future.* Each work has been tagged with the child's data specifying age, place of birth, length of stay in Poland, year of schooling, contact with Polish language outside

---

2 Ordinance of the Minister of National Education dated February 14, 2017 on the core curriculum for preschool education and the core curriculum for general education for elementary school, including students with moderate or severe intellectual disabilities, general education for a Vocational school of the first degree, general education for a special school for special education and general education for a post-secondary school (Journal of Laws 2017, item 356), p. 1.

3 Cf. in this publication chap. by Lucyna Warda-Radys.

4 https://korpus-foko.ug.edu.pl/index.php?page=11.

of school[5], and the corpus search engine allows filtering the works due to the criteria given above. The collected material shows the linguistic difficulties of students with the experience of migration, and reveals the problems underlying communicative misunderstandings. The corpus material can also be used to identify the types and ranges of difficulties faced by Polish teachers working in multilingual and multicultural classrooms[6].

The analysis of dozens of works by Ukrainian and Belarusian students shows how the phenomenon of intercomprehension can allow teachers to understand the written works of children at different levels of (in)knowledge of Polish[7]. At the same time, it is important to note the difficulties associated with the lack of knowledge of the Russian and Ukrainian alphabet by many teachers, which significantly hinders access to electronic translation support tools. A detailed analysis of selected works, will show what difficulties teachers and students of Polish studies face.

This article will present only one aspect of the work of a Polish language teacher – the development of students' lexical competence[8] – will be discussed from the perspective of the teacher in the context of the phenomenon of inter-comprehension.[9]

Working on the development of students' vocabulary is one of the most important tasks of a teacher in the lessons of native and foreign languages, an

---

5   The sociolinguistic data was collected in compliance with the principles of the RODO and does not allow for the identification of the author of the paper.

6   In cooperation with the Pomeranian Teachers' Center in Gdansk, a series of webinars were recorded to show the possibilities of working with the "FoKo" corpus: https://www.youtube.com/playlist?list=PLtjLJZYAwuTfncPZWsLgiiLb9F67SBHF9.

7   In 2010 the Center for the Development of Education in Poland published Krystyna M. Błeszyńska's report on her research into the situation of foreign children in Polish schools. Although, as the author notes, the number of migrants and foreign students in Polish schools was not yet significant at the time, "the evaluation/price of the existing situation was to be used to design measures aimed at effectively supporting the development and social integration of foreign children, both younger and older" (Błeszyńska 2010). The intention was to prepare Polish educational institutions for the challenges of increasing migration in Europe. In the following decade, the presence of children with migrant experience in Polish schools became more and more visible, and the local governments of cities where the number of migrants reached a significant scale undertook various initiatives to support education, e. g., in Gdansk, on the initiative of ex-president Pawel Adamowicz, an Integration Model of Immigrants was developed (https://www.gdansk.pl/laczy-nas-gdansk/faq-model-integracji?lang=pl), prepared in many substantive teams (including education), a guidebook *Inny w polskiej szkole (A stranger at Polish School)* was published in Warsaw in 2010 (https://edukacja.um.warszawa.pl/edukacja-dla-cudzoziemcow). Similar projects were undertaken in many Polish cities.

8   Anna Seretny (2015) devoted a comprehensive monograph to this topic: *Słownictwo w dydaktyce języka. Świat słów na przykładzie języka polskiego jako obcego.* (Vocabulary in the didactics of language. The world of words on the example of Polish as a foreign language.)

9   On intercomprehension in the aspect of understanding the works of children studying in Polish schools, cf. also Lucyna Warda-Radys.

important part of this task is the feedback that students receive from the teacher checking students' written statements.

The study is a case study and was based on the analysis of one essay presented in the "FoKo" Corpus. The selected work reveals a number of problems related to the phenomenon of intercomprehension: syntactic, inflectional and lexical. The subject of attention in this study will be primarily the difficulties of the text sender in searching for Polish words that would allow him to name what he wants to write about. The lexical deficiencies in Polish and the sense of kinship between Polish and Russian language result in the transcription with the Polish alphabet of words taken from Russian, and this in turn makes it difficult for the Polish teacher to understand the text accurately and to formulate correct feedback that could help the student develop her lexical stock.

The analised work was written by a thirteen-year-old[10] girl born in Belarus (after 16 months in Poland), studying at Year 7, for whom the home language and the language of education was Russian for twelve years. The phenomenon of intercomprehension, understood as "a form of communication in which each person uses his or her own language and understands the utterances of the others" (Doyé 2004: 60) without deliberate study or additional effort (European Commission 2012: 1) should make it easier for a Polish language teacher to understand the student's essay, but as the following analysis will show in a school situation, such superficial understanding of the text is insufficient.

Although there are still teachers working in Polish education, who learnt Russian (which was a compulsory subject in Poland until 1990[11]) for many years of their education, the majority of teachers employed in school today, as well as students of Polish language who studies specialising in teaching, do not know Russian and have never learned it.

The survey was conducted among teachers – students of the postgraduate course Teaching Polish as a Foreign Language and students of Polish philology at the University of Gdansk, 57% of respondents submitted that they had not learned any Slavic language before.

50 questionnaires prepared in the Microsoft Forms tool were sent out, checking the understanding of the essay by teachers and students of Polish philology from the teaching faculty specialty. The questionnaire included a scan of the original essay. The command addressed to the respondents was in the following form:

---

10 The age of the student was given on the basis of a questionnaire filled out by the teacher, in the essay the virtual sender states that she is 15 years old, from the data provided by the teacher it appears that the student is 13 years old.

11 On teaching Russian in Poland, cf. e. g. Figarski 2008.

Please transform the given text of the student essay.

Please change erroneous forms and words to correct ones, change the sentence formation if necessary. Please change foreign words to Polish words. In place of words or forms that you do not understand (do not know what to replace them with), please leave blank dotted spaces […]. If you are not sure whether the proposed change is correct, please put a question mark in parentheses (?) next to the correction.

THE STUDY IS ABOUT INTUITIVE UNDERSTANDING, SO PLEASE DO NOT USE DICTIONARIES AND TRANSALATORS.

The respondents received a scan of the text, which is not available in the Corpus "FoKo"[12], it is visible only in the resources to the authors of the Corpus. It was decided to use the scan because it reproduces a natural teaching situation.

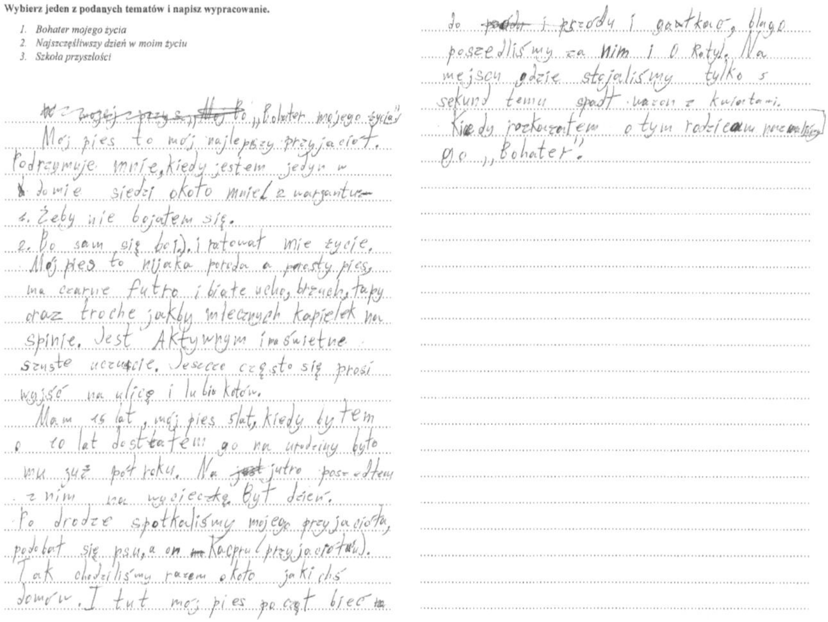

Wybierz jeden z podanych tematów i napisz wypracowanie.

1. Bohater mojego życia
2. Najszczęśliwszy dzień w moim życiu
3. Szkoła przyszłości

Figure 1: A scan of an essay written by a thirteen-year-old, grade 7 student of a Polish elementary school, after a 16-month stay in Poland.

The "Foko" corpus includes the text transcribed in TXT format in accordance with the accepted rules for editing collected manuscript texts:

---

12 In a database that has a large reach, potentially also among students, for reasons of data protection, we present transcribed texts (according to the editing rules given on the project website: https://korpus-foko.ug.edu.pl/index.php?page=6). Editing the texts electronically will also enable further IT operations on the texts.

dnia 01.12.2021 r.

"Bohater mojego życia". Mój pies to mój najlepszy przyjaciół. Podrzymuje mnie, kiedy jestem jedyn w domie siedzi około mnie (2 warjantu: 1. Żeby nie bojałem się. 2. Bo sam się boi.). i ratował mie życie. Mój pies to nijaka poroda a prosty pies, ma czarne futro i białe ucho, brzuch, łapy oraz troche jakby mlecznych kapielek na spinie. Jest Aktywnym i ma świetne szuste uczucie. Jeszcze często się prosi wyjść na ulicę i lubi kotów. Mam 15 lat, mój pies 5 lat, kiedy byłem o 10 lat dostałem go na urodziny było mu już pół roku. Na jutro poszedłem z nim na wycieczkę. Był dzień. Po drodze spotkaliśmy mojego przyjacióła, podobał się psu, a on Kacpru (przyjaciółu). Tak chodziliśmy razem około jakichś domów. I tut mój pies po czął bieć do pszódu i gałkać, blago poszedliśmy za nim i O Rety!. Na mejscu gdzie stojaliśmy tylko 5 sekund temu spadł wazon z kwiatami. Kiedy rozkazałem o tym rodzicam nazwaliśmy go "Bohater" (K 296)[13]

dated 01/12/2021.

"The hero of my life. My dog is my best friend. It holds me up when I am one in the house, sits around me (2 variants: 1. So that I am not afraid. 2. Because it is afraid itself.). And saved my life. My dog is a nondescript breed dog but an ordinary dog, it has black fur and white ear, belly, paws and a little like milk drippings on the spin. It is an active and has a great sixth sense. It still often asks to go out on the street and likes cats. I am 15 years old, my dog is 5 years old, when I was about 10 years old I got him for my birthday, he was already six months old. For tomorrow I went on a trip with him. It was daytime. On the way we met my friend, liked the dog and it liked Kacpru (friend). We walked together around some houses. Suddenly my dog started to run to the front and barking, so we followed him and Oh Gosh! At the place where we were standing only for 5 seconds, a vase with flowers fell. When I told my parents about it, we named it "Hero" (K 296)

The subject of this analysis will be the scanned original essay (Figure 1.) and 50 texts edited by the survey respondents.

The essay selected for the study perfectly illustrates the research problem undertaken. It reveals the student's difficulties in mastering Polish (in terms of linguistic production) related to various aspects of second language acquisition and learning, but a preliminary analysis allows us to assume that teachers reading the essay will also have difficulties in accurately understanding the text at the level of the lexical layer. After all, the teacher needs to understand the text accurately, decoding the meaning of each word, to be able to give the student feedback on her lexical choices.

The student used 20 different verbs in the paper, including two that may be incomprehensible to an audience unfamiliar with Russian: *gałkać, razkazałem*. Out of 27 nouns used in the paper, the following may be incomprehensible to the recipient: *poroda, kapielki, spina,* in addition, the adverb *tut*, adjectives *prosty* i *nijaka*. In the essay also appeared a form that is difficult for the recipient to

---

13 The code of the work in accordance with the coding in the "FoKo" corpus.

identify: *siedzi kolo mnie z / 2 wariantu*. Thus, the difficulties concern a small percentage of the text, but important in the reception, important for the teacher, who assesses the communicative competence of the student[14], especially his lexical resource and choice of words appropriate to the cognitive and stylistic requirements of the constructed text.

The survey confirmed the occurrence of difficulties in understanding the text in the passages indicated above. In the 50 texts received in the survey, various strategies were used to deal with unintelligible places: dots were repeatedly inserted or the difficult places mentioned above were omitted, but the text was also transformed, choosing in place of foreign words and expressions their Polish equivalents. These were many times literal translations of the Russian word, but words with a different meaning, but similar to the word from the essay in graphic form, were also given (e. g. poroda – petarda), sometimes respondents in place of the foreign word gave two Polish words according to them contextually corresponding to the Russian word. By making transformations of the text included in the survey, the respondents revealed their semantic and stylistic choices. Therefore, it can be expected that they would provide such feedback to their students.

Places that proved difficult to understand in the analised text were the underlined words and phrases in the following passages: *Podrzymuje mnie, kiedy jestem jedyn w domie siedzi około mnie /2 warjantu: 1. Żeby nie bojałem się. 2. Bo sam się boi.); Mój pies to **nijaka poroda a prosty pies**, ma czarne futro i białe ucho, brzuch, łapy oraz troche jakby mlecznych **kapielek na spinie**; Jest Aktywnym i ma* świetne **szuste uczu**cie; **I tut** mój pies po czął bieć do pszódu i **gałkać**; *Kiedy* **rozkazałem** *o tym rodzicam.*

> It holds me up when I am one in the house, sits around me / 2 variants: 1. So that I am not afraid. 2. Because it is afraid itself.). My dog is a nondescript breed dog but an ordinary dog, it has black fur and white ear, belly, paws and a little like milk drippings on the spin. It is an active and has a great sixth sense. Suddenly my dog started to run to the front and barking; When I told my parents about it.

They will be discussed in this particular order.

Part 2 *warjantu* was most often left dotted by the survey participants – as many as 84% of the respondents. There were also two phrases selected on the basis of

---

14 School essays are a very important instrument for training a student's linguistic competence. Agnieszka Rypel lists the 4 most important functions that a student's written statement has: didactic, educational, diagnostic and expressive (2004, pp. 313–314). In the context of this study, the didactic function is of primary importance. "The writing of school texts serves primarily to practise linguistic and textual skills," writes A. Rypel – supports the formation of the student's personal style, in addition, it has a pragmatic dimension – especially in terms of the so-called applied forms, the mastery of which prepares the student to participate in social and professional life" (2004, p. 313).

addition unrelated to the meaning of the unrecognised word: *siedzi merdając, siedzi zazwyczaj inconsistent* (sits wagging, sits usually) with the intention of the sender, but possible in a text about a dog. Only three times this text was replaced as follows: *z wyboru* (by choice) and three times – *z powodu* (because of).

The Russian word вариант is Polish word 'wariant' (WSRP, WUSRJ)), also meaning 'option, possibility'. Phrases such as: Есть вариант(ы) with the meaning 'there are various options, e. g. solutions to the problem' are very common in the language, Какой вариант ты предлагаешь? (What option do you propose?)[15]. Therefore, the closest answers to this meaning were those in which the fragment *z/2 of the variant* was replaced with the expression *z powodu* because of.

Almost as many difficulties were caused by the denunciation *Mój pies to nijaka poroda a prosty pies* (My dog is a nondescript breed dog but an ordinary dog). The word poroda was replaced by dots, leaving the space blank, by 14 respondents (28%), but as many as 33 people transformed the text in accordance with the meaning of порода – Russian 'breed' (cf. WSRP, i. e. 2, cf. also Glosbe)[16], making various syntactic transformations of the denunciation from the student's work, accurately conveying the meaning of the whole statement, e. g.: *Mój pies nie jest rasowy, lecz zwyczajny. Moj pies nie jest rasowy (zadna rasa?), a zwykly pies, Nie ma rasy – to zwykly pies* (My dog is not purebred, but an ordinary. My dog is not a breed (no breed?), but an ordinary dog, There is no breed – it's an ordinary dog), in which the noun *rasa* (a breed) or the adjective *rasowy* (breed) appeared 33 times, including one use of the colloquial lexeme breeder (cf. WSJP breeder). The respondents replaced the expression *prosty pies* (a simple dog) most often with the expression *zwykly pies* (an ordinary dog) (15 uses), twice with the phrase *jest zwyczajny* (is ordinary), once with the expression *zwyczajny pies* (ordinary dog), twice reached for the expressions *zwykły kundel / zwykły kundelek* (ordinary little mongrel), three times used the word *kundel* (mongrel) without the attributive *zwykły* (ordinary) and twice with the word kundelek (little mongrel), once occurred the word *mieszaniec* and once the colloquial word *nierasowiec* (no-breed). The expression *zwykły pies* (simple dog) was left out of the Polish version eight times, a sign that the close affinity of the languages can lead to a loss of linguistic sense. Simple written in the Polish alphabet refers to

---

15 Possibly influenced by English, see https://context.reverso.net/перевод/русский-англий ский/есть+вариант.

16 In addition to scholarly dictionaries, the article uses the Glosbe online dictionary, since it is a tool available to Polish teachers that allows them to check meanings immediately, when dictionaries are difficult to access. It is worth noting, however, that this tool, like Google translator, will not recognise a Russian word written in Polish letters poroda. Using this tool requires transcription of the foreign word from the student's work into the Russian alphabet, cf. https://pl.glosbe.com/ru/pl/порода, which cannot be expected of teachers unfamiliar with Russian.

Russian простой in the 2nd meaning 'zwyczajny' (ordinary) (cf. WSRP), which is closest to the 3rd meaning of the Polish adjective *prosty* 'niewyróżniający się spośród innych' (WSJP) (indistinguishable from others). However, according to the WSJP, only in combination with the noun *człowiek* (man). The expression *prosty pies* (simple dog) in the sense of 'pies neirasowy' (non-breed dog) does not occur in Polish, yet 16 percent of surveyed native speakers of Polish, teachers and students of Polish studies, left this expression. 3 surveys also left the expression *nijaka rasa* (neuter breed?), probably suggesting not the Russian никакой i.e. 1. 'żaden' (WSRP) (none), but the Polish adjective *nijaki* (neuter), which, although it had the meaning 'żaden' (none) in old Polish (WSJP 2. 'żaden'), is no longer used in modern times. *Nijaki* today i.e. 1. is 'pozbawiony cech charakterystycznych i wyrazistych' (WSJP) ('devoid of distinctive and distinctive features', so it cannot be used in conjunction with the lexeme race, where distinctive features appear in the definition: 'odmiana hodowlana określonego zwierzęcia wyróżniająca się przekazywanymi dziedzicznie <u>charakterystycznymi cechami budowy</u>, wyglądu i zachowania' (WSJP) (a breeding variety of a particular animal distinguished by hereditarily transmitted characteristic features of conformation, appearance and behaviour). It is also interesting to note the use of this word by the author – a Russian-speaking girl, but of Belarusian origin). It seems likely that the student, despite declaring in the questionnaire that she does not speak Belarusian, uses Belarusian words in her transition to Polish, since it seems to her that Belarusian words are closer to Polish than the corresponding Russian words[17] and therefore in her work she uses the word ніякі, which in Belarusian has precisely the meaning – 'żaden' (Glosbe)

Another explanation for the use of the Polish words *nijaka* (poroda) and *prosty* (pies –dog) in the studied essay by both the author and the authors of the transformations may be the trap of "false friends of the translator." Polish speakers in particular, reading a text saturated with russicism, were fooled by the translator's false friends and left words familiar to them from Polish, losing the linguistic sense proper to native speakers.

Occasionally, respondents replaced the Russianisms present in the statement with other words or Polish expressions close in meaning to the expressions *żadna rasa, zwyczajny pies* e.g.: *Mój pies to <u>nic nadzwyczajnego</u>* (1 użycie), nie <u>jest nadzwyczajnym psem</u> (My dog is nothing extraordinary (1 usage), he is not an extraordinary dog). Once appeared in the questionnaires a word with a completely inadequate meaning for the expression *żadna rasa* (no race), selected probably on the basis of the graphic proximity of the Polish transcription of the

---

17 The text was consulted with Tatiana Kananowicz, Ph.D., professor at the University of Gdansk, who notes this phenomenon when working with Belarussian students and pupils living in Poland.

russianism *poroda* and the lexeme *petarda: Mój pies to żadna petarda* (My dog is no firecracker).

The second segment of the phrase in question – *ma czarne futro i białe ucho, brzuch, łapy oraz troche jakby mlecznych kapielek na spinie* (he has black fur and white ears, belly, paws and a bit like milky drippings on a spin) – included the expression *kapielki na spinie*, which was incomprehensible to many who filled out the survey. Thus, the lexeme *kapielki* was omitted 15 times, but more often it was replaced by words that were appropriate in meaning: *kropelki* (droplets) – 18 uses, *plamki* (spots) – 9 uses, *łatki* (patches) – 4 uses. The Russian word капелька is the Polish 'kropelka' (WSRP), and these substitutions were the most in the survey, perhaps determined by the use of this very word's graphic association with the Polish verb 'kapać', and perhaps further association – *kapią kropelki* (drip drops). Although the words *plamki* (spots) and *łatki* (patches) do not correspond to the meaning of the Russian капелька, contextually they are appropriate, and such feedback should be given to the student. After all, in Polish, the connection *mleczne kropelki na grzbiecie* (milky dots on the back) can be considered a metaphorical term for the dog's coat, but the following connections would be apt and natural: *mleczne plamki, łatki, cętki* (milky spots, patches, spots).

Twice at this point in the text there were expressions that completely do not correspond to the textual meaning: *kremowe łapy* (cream paws).

The word *spina*, Russian спина 'plecy' (WSRP) (a back), was equally difficult for respondents. *Plecy*, however, was used in only 2 surveys, the most common was the contextually appropriate *grzbiet* (a back) (13 uses), and the Polish word *kręgosłup* (a spine)[18] was used four times. However, the connections *plamki na kręgosłupie* psa (speckled on a dog's spine) should be considered incorrect in Polish when referring to the description of its coat. As many as 28 respondents dotted this word without giving a Polish equivalent, 5 people gave – probably guessing – *ogon* (tail), 2 people – pysk (muzzle).

Understanding the phrase *szuste czucie* also proved difficult, despite the fact that the phrase corresponding to the Russian шестое чувство (WUSRJ) phrase *szósty zmysł* (sixth sense) is, after all, common in Polish. The meaning of this phrase is related to the global understanding of the text, which is why such a large number of blanks is surprising. The climax of the story was based precisely on the fact that the dog was endowed with this sixth sense and thus saved the boys. However, the Polish version of the expression *szuste czucie* – szósty zmysł appeared only in 16 surveys but in 18 the place was dotted. Six texts used other

---

18 It is worth mentioning that in an interview with respondents conducted after the collection of the text surveys, many students explained that they guessed the meaning of the word spina by associating it with the English spine 'spine' (Glosbe).

expressions or phrases close in meaning to the expression sixth sense: *szósty zmysł: (świetnie) odczytuje uczucia,* (ma) *świetne wyczucie, świetny instynkt* [(great) reads feelings, (has) great feeling, great instinct, once with the addition of hunting] – *łowiecki* – (ma) *instynkt łowiecki* [(has) hunting instinct]. Many respondents (9 people) suggested the similarity of the word – *czucie* (feel) to the Polish noun *uczucie* (feeling) and the verb *czuć* (feel), so there appeared in the answers of respondents the forms: *czyste uczucie, czyste uczucia, świetne, czyste? uczucie, szóste uczucie* (pure feeling, pure feelings, great, pure? feeling, sixth feeling) and expressions built on this association: (jest) *czułym zwierzęciem, odczuwa szczęście,* (ma) *dobre serce, bardzo kochany* [(is) a tender animal, feels happiness, has a good heart, very loved].

The graphic proximity of the Belarusian girl's use of the lexeme 'tut' with Polish words determined the decision to replace the Russianized тут i. e. 2 'at that time' (WSRP) used in the paper with Polish functional expressions: *tu* (4 uses) and *tutaj* (3 uses) cf WSJP. The idiomatic expression и тут – 'nagle' (suddenly) was accurately rendered by the Polish *nagle* (suddenly) by 18 respondents, 5 – gave another Polish equivalent, – *wtedy* (then), 3 people – *w tym momencie* (at that moment), 1 person – *potem* (then) all also consistent with the meaning noted in the Russian-Polish dictionary. Ten survey participants omitted the phrase.

A lot of difficulties were provided by another russianism to the respondents: *gałkać* – Russian гавкать 'szczekać' (WSRP, Glosbe) (to bark), in 21 surveys it was replaced by the Polish equivalent – *szczekać* (to bark), but omitted in as many as 28, in one it was inserted: *skakać* (to jump), in one a comment was added: 'out of context'. The latter comment in particular is interesting; it implies that in this case the context does not help in understanding the russification used. Also interesting is the student's use of the Polish letter ł in place of [w]: гавкать. The sound [w] has been replaced by the Belarusian/Polish [ł], perhaps influenced by the didactic actions of teachers, who often focus on this phonetic (and graphic) problem when teaching students for whom Russian or Ukrainian is the native language.

The lexeme *rozkazałem* (Russian: рассказать 'opowiedzieć' WSRP; (to tell) was replaced by the word I told in 30 surveys, 17 used the Polish equivalent *powiedziałem* (I said), and omitted the word only three times. Contextually accurate are both the lexeme *opowiedziałem* (I told) and *powiedziałem* (I said), so it can be assumed that the authors of the transformations chose the Polish equivalent of the foreign word from the essay on the basis of contextual re-construction of the meaning of the unknown word.

The fivefold use of the negated form *nie lubi (kotów)* (dislikes cats) in place of the phrase *lubi kotów* (likes cats) used in the paper also proved interesting. This is probably due to the suggestion of Polish syntax, in which the genitive appears in the negated forms of verbs here: *nie lubić czego?* (do not like anything?), and the accusative in non-denial forms, here: *lubić co?* like what? However, the student's work shows the influence of the Russian paradigm, where in the plural of vital nouns the accusative is equal to the genitive. This example illustrates the complexity of mutual interference of related languages in the process of learning a language and understanding texts produced in a related language. Consequently, the phenomenon of intercomprehension led 5 recipients of the content to misunderstand the meaning and assume that the protagonist of the story read – "pies nie lubi kotów," (the dog does not like cats), when the intention of the sender was to express the opposite meaning – 'pies lubi koty' (the dog likes cats).

The analysis of the understanding of Polish teachers and students of the teaching specialty of the Gdansk Polish language department of the Belarusian schoolgirl's difficult places showed that, although the phenomenon of intercomprehension supports the global understanding of the text, but in the situation of school didactics this proves insufficient.

All of the Polish language and literature students surveyed in their edits conveyed the surface sense of the text, even if they omitted some parts of the original. However, with regard to school didactics, this is not a fully sufficient mechanism for two reasons. First, because the sender of the text, the student, for whom Polish is a second language and at the same time the language of school education, strives to give his thoughts the most accurate linguistic shape possible, in accordance with the norm of the language he is learning. In the essay in question, the sender wrote about his favourite, hero dog, introduced him to the recipient, so he wanted to reproduce him well linguistically. The recipient should decode all the elements of meaning, imagine the dog's colouring, understand that he had extraordinary abilities to sense danger. Many recipients, unfortunately, did not understand precisely these important details, and thus could not give the student correct feedback on how these intentions should be correctly expressed by the sender in Polish.

The survey revealed different approaches of the surveyed teachers and Polish language students to the student's text. In carrying out the instructions, the respondents transformed the text (Please transform the given text of the student's essay) so that it conformed to the norm with (Please change erroneous forms and words to correct ones, change the sentence formation if necessary) and changed borrowed words to their Polish equivalents (Foreign words please change to Polish words).

The collected performances of these instructions showed the use of different editorial strategies adopted for a text that is not fully understood. The first approach is to omit the unintelligible word and leave a gap (in accordance with the instructions to the respondents). Such a procedure makes the teacher aware that he or she is not reading the meaning of the word and must use other means than intercomprehension to recognize the meaning of a foreign word, such as consulting dictionaries. The second strategy is to replace a foreign word with its Polish exact equivalent, even though in Polish the word translated exactly does not have such a range of connectivity, e. g. *mleczne kapielki na spinie – mleczne kropelki na grzbiecie* is an expression that a native speaker of Polish would not use. Such transformations of the text can lead to erroneous feedback. After all, the student should receive full feedback from the teacher – on the meaning of the word *kapielka*, but also on its connectivity in Polish [e. g., kropelka rosy, wody (dewdrop, water, etc.] and a suggestion as to what words and expressions should be used to describe the dog's coat – and this, the third strategy, was adopted by many of the respondents, transforming the passage in such a way: *mleczne plamki/łatki na grzbiecie* (milky spots/patches on the back).

This is because the teacher should be aware that a mental lexicon is "not only a person's memorized collection of lexemes, but also his intuitive knowledge of the various semantic-structural relations occurring between these words, as well as his knowledge of the semantic, syntactic, phonological and orthographic aspects of the words that constitute this mental lexicon (Kurcz 2005, 119). Developing a student's vocabulary teaches not only new words, gives their meanings, but also shows their use in connections that are natural to the Polish language. An excellent tool, simple to use in any lesson, can be the online *Wielki słownik języka polski*ego (where there-https://wsjp.pl), where a Connections tab (Połączenia) is placed next to each headword (cf. for example, the headwords *łatka* i *plamka*), where the student (and teacher) will find many connections[19] typical of the Polish language.

Another approach to difficult places is to replace unfamiliar words with other words, according to the author of the transformation, such words that could be found in a given context, although they testify to a misunderstanding of the original word, e. g. in place of the original *siedzi około mnie (2 warjantu* (sits around me (2 warjantu) proposes– *siedzi merdając, siedzi zazwyczaj, gałkać – skakać* (sits merry, sits usually, gałkać – jump).

This should be considered an attempt to avoid difficult places, rather than an effort to understand the speech of the sender of the text. such actions can also prove useful in giving feedback to the student, because they show the possibilities of developing the text, introducing more new words into it, and therefore new meanings.

Using the method of transforming the student's text proposed in the questionnaire in the daily work of a polonist and creating the teacher's own editing of the student's work can prove to be an interesting proposal for enriching the teacher's workshop. It will allow the teacher not only to recognize the lexical

---

19 https://wsjp.pl/haslo/podglad/7508/latka/5208136/plamka, https://wsjp.pl/haslo/podglad/36 131/kropelka/4558644/wody.

deficiencies of the student, but naturally leads to the creation of a text in which in place of foreign words (but also incorrect grammatical and syntactic forms) will appear correct Polish equivalents, which can later be used in formulating feedback to the student.

The teacher should also use his knowledge of language and linguistic awareness to recognize the mechanism of the student's error, choose the correct Polish form and appropriate teaching actions to teach it.

The analysis of fifty texts presented above showed how difficult this task is. Polonists and students of Polish studies have repeatedly made wrong choices, e. g., they have stooped to accurate translations of the Russian word, despite the fact that it does not occur in Polish in such meanings, e. g., *prosty pies* – 'kundel' (simple dog – 'mongrel'), changed the affirmative form to the negated one, without recognising the syntactic and inflectional mechanisms (in a sense of syntactic requirements of the verb and meaning of the noun) – *nie lubi kotów* (does not like cats).

Intercomprehension allows students and teachers of multilingual classes to understand each other in everyday school communication, but the work of a Polish language teacher teaching Polish in a multilingual classroom is not enough. Knowledge and linguistic awareness are needed, as well as adequate didactic competence.

In the didactic work, not only numerous textbooks for teaching Polish as a foreign language, but also materials related to the teaching of Polish as a first language can be of help to the teacher. In the context of the problems discussed above, Regina Pawlowska's monograph *Metodyka ćwiczeń w czytaniu* (2002) (Methods of Exercising in Reading) is worth recommending, especially the chapter entitled *Metody pracy nad znaczeniem wyrazu* (Methods of Working on the Meaning of Words).

A case study – an analysis of one paper and its fifty transformations revealed how much information can be gained by analising a student's paper and how many challenges are faced today by teachers working in a Polish school that has changed rapidly from a monolingual and monocultural school to a multilingual and multicultural school.

Bibliography

Bełszyńska E. (2010), *Dzieci obcokrajowców w polskich placówkach oświatowych – perspektywa szkoły. Raport z badan´*, Warszawa.

Dołowy-Rybińsk N. (2004), *Interkomprehensja języków słowiańskich jako czynnik motywujący do uczenia się języka górnołużyckiego dla uczniów Gimnazjum Górnołużyckiego pochodzących z niemieckojęzycznych rodzin*, "Zeszyty Łużyckie" 55, s. 299–318.

Doyé P. (2004), *A Methodological Framework for the Teaching of Intercompre-hension*, "Language Learning Journal" 30 (1), 59–68.

Figarski W. (2008), *Język rosyjski w Polsce – fakty i mity*, "Przegląd Rusycystyczny" nr 1 (121), s. 84–97.

Kurcz I. (2005), *Psychologia języka i komunikacji*, Warszawa.

Pawłowska R. (2002), *Metodyka ćwiczeń w czytaniu*, Gdańsk.

Rypel A., *Język pisany w szkole – między kreatywnością a schematem*, [w:] *Językowe literackie i kulturowe ścieżki edukacji polonistycznej (tradycja i współczesność)*, Katowice 2014.

Seretny A. (2015), *Słownictwo w dydaktyce języka. Świat słów na przykładzie języka polskiego jako obcego*, Warszawa 2015.

Netography

https://korpus-foko.ug.edu.pl/index.php?page=3

https://samorzad.pap.pl/kategoria/edukacja/mein-w-polskich-szkolach-i-przedszkolach-jest-1879-tys-dzieci-i-mlodziezy-z

https://um.warszawa.pl/waw/wcies/-/zespol-ds-nauczania-dzieci-cudzoziemskich

https://wsjp.pl/#

https://www.gdansk.pl/migracje/model-integracji-imigrantow,a,61064

https://www.nik.gov.pl/plik/id,22685,vp,25384.pdf

https://www.gazetaprawna.pl/wiadomosci/kraj/artykuly/9440304,men-w-systemie-edukacji-mamy-ponad-180-tys-dzieci-i-mlodziezy-z-ukra.html

https://pl.glosbe.com

Legal acts

Ordinance of the Minister of National Education dated February 14, 2017 on the core curriculum for preschool education and the core curriculum for general education of elementary school, including students with moderate or severe intellectual disabilities, general education for an industrial school of the first degree, general education for a special school for special education and general education for a post-secondary school (Journal of Laws 2017, item 356), p. 1.

Solution of abbreviations

WSJP – *Wielki słownik języka polskiego*, red. P. Żmigrodzki, https://wsjp.pl

WUSRJ – Большой универсальный словарь русского языка, Moskwa, 2016.

WSRP –*Wielki słownik rosyjsko-polski z kluczem polsko-rosyjskim*, red. J. Wawrzyńczak, Warszawa 2004.

Lucyna Warda-Radys (University of Gdańsk)

Teacher's work with a Slavic child with migrant experience in the perspective of intercomprehension

Abstract

In view of the increasing 'internationalisation' of lower-level education in Poland (especially after Russia's aggression against Ukraine in February 2022), it seems necessary to collect data and conduct research on the language of adolescents with family migration experience. Identifying the linguistic needs of such pupils can be an important step towards increasing their educational opportunities in the Polish school system. A response to these research needs is the 'FoKo' Learner Corpus of Polish Language (https://korpus-foko.ug.ed u.pl), established at the Faculty of Philology of the University of Gdansk, which collects the works of people learning Polish as a foreign/second language. Its methodological assumption was to collect a written works obtained from children and adoloscents with current migration experience studying in primary and secondary schools. The students' work collected in the corpus shows their level of proficiency in Polish, primarily in terms of writing skills, but it is also accompanied by questionnaires completed by teachers that relate to other language skills. These data allow us to conclude that for the rapid adaptation of foreign-language learners to the Polish educational system and equipping them with the linguistic competence to acquire knowledge in Polish, intercultural solutions should prove useful and effective.

There has been a growing amount of recent research into the language of foreigners learning Polish, particularly with regard to the mistakes they make. There are both cross-sectional works involving studies of the language of groups of students with different L1[1], as well as more detailed analyses of the difficulties of a

---

1 Cf. e. g., A. Dąbrowska, *Najczęstsze błędy popełniane przez cudzoziemców uczących się języka polskiego jako obcego*, w: Opisywanie, rozwijanie i testowanie znajomości języka polskiego jako obcego. Materiały z konferencji sekcji glottodydaktycznej Stowarzyszenia "Bristol" Polskich i Zagranicznych Nauczycieli Kultury Polskiej i Języka Polskiego jako Obcego [Most Frequent Mistakes Made by Foreigners Learning Polish as a Foreign Language, in: Describing, Developing and Testing Knowledge of Polish as a Foreign Language. Materials from the conference of the glottodidactic section of the Bristol Association of Polish and Foreign Teachers of Polish Culture and Language as a Foreign Language], ed. A. Seretny, W. Martyniuk, E. Lipinska, Krakow 2004, pp. 105–136.

specific group of students with a single native language[2], or even just of a selected type of error made by such students[3]. This research has been and continues to be carried out among adults, mainly foreign-language students of Polish studies in various countries or candidates to study at Polish universities, learning Polish on various types of shorter or longer language courses. To date, however, no analysis has been made of the language spoken by the under-age students[4] (children and adolescents), who recently (and especially after the start of the Russian aggression against Ukraine in February 2022) have appeared en masse in Polish schools – both primary and secondary – and whose presence has recently become one of the major challenges the Polish educational system faces. In order to be able to implement effective methods of teaching and educational work with such pupils (with appropriately adapted content and the necessary support), it is necessary to not only understand the complexity of their experiences and specific functioning, but also to diagnose their level of language competence. Adequate recognition of the language needs of such pupils can be the first step in improving their educational opportunities. In view of this progressive 'internationalisation' of lower secondary education in Poland, data collection and research on the language of under-age pupils with family migration experience therefore seems necessary[5].

These are the works of pupils aged between 10 and 19, mostly collected among: 1) children who came to Poland from Ukraine (but also from Belarus, Moldova or Kazakhstan) and for whom Ukrainian or Russian is their first language; 2) Polish re-migrant children who returned to Poland after a period of emigration after starting school in the educational system of another country (most often in the United Kingdom or Ireland); and 3) children with a Polish cultural background

---

2 See, for example. Górska A., *Błędy studentów z Ukrainy – zapobieganie i eliminacja w grupach o zróżnicowanych możliwościach (na podstawie doświadczeń Centrum Partnerstwa Wschodniego Uniwersytetu Opolskiego)* [Errors of Ukrainian Students – Prevention and Elimination in Groups with Different Abilities (based on the experience of the Centre for Eastern Partnership of the University of Opole)], "Acta Universitatis Lodziensis", 2015, pp. 357–370; Kaczmarska E., Zasina A. J.: *Język polski w tekstach osób czeskojęzycznych na podstawie korpusu uczniowskiego PoLKo* [Polish in the Texts of Czech Speakers on the Basis of the PoLKo Student Corpus], "Rossica Olomucensia. Časopis pro ruskou a slovanskou filologii", 2021, LX, pp. 5–17.

3 Cf. Krawczuk A., 2009, *Błędy leksykalne i leksykalno-stylistyczne w polszczyźnie Ukraińców* [Lexical and Lexical-Stylistic Errors in the Polish Language of Ukrainians], "Postscriptum Polonistyczne" [Polish Postscriptum] No. 1(3), pp. 167–183; Kaczmarska E., Zasina A. J.: *Błędy walencyjne w tekstach obcokrajowców uczących się języka polskiego w świetle korpusu PoLKo.* [Valency Errors in the Texts of Foreigners Learning Polish in the Light of the PoLKo Corpus.] "Prace Filologiczne", [Philological Works] 2020, 75, pp. 197–213.

4 In particular, the researchers point out the difficulty in obtaining research material from this group of people.

5 The language of students who are Polish citizens returning with their parents from emigration deserves similar attention.

attending Polish weekend schools abroad[6]. The collected material consists of essays (creative school stories) written on one of the three given subjects[7] (with no indication of the required length of the text), as well as statements supplementing balloons in several comic drawings presenting various everyday communicative situations requiring specific polite behaviour (e.g. an apology, a request, an invitation). The value of the collected material is that the papers were written by children and young people by hand and under the guidance of a teacher, and therefore without correction prompted by electronic devices. In addition, questionnaires containing sociolinguistic data and an interview about the child's language situation before arriving in Poland and the current one, after arriving in our country, have been collected by the teachers. To date, the works of more than 300 students have been collected. The period of their stay in Poland until the time of the research performance shows a wide span, as does the level of their educational background (and the resulting different levels of competence in their mother tongue) and their level of knowledge of Polish (children who do not know Polish at all and those who learned Polish in their country of origin or at home because they come from families with Polish roots) and other Slavic and non-Slavic languages (children from multicultural and multilingual families).

The environment for the presentation of the corpus is the platform of the University of Gdansk, where a special programme[8] has been developed for the corpus, enabling searches by different criteria (gender, age, country of birth, length of stay in Poland and class at a Polish school). As the corpus was conceived as a tool to be used in the future by both teachers of Polish schools and researchers dealing with the acquisition of Polish as a foreign language, two parallel ways of presenting the material have been planned. Access to the former is open. This view presents the works in their pure form, as it was developed by the students in the final version. In the view designed for the exploration of linguistic material for research purposes, the transcribed text is enriched with markers of corrections that were applied by the authors of the texts. The system of these tags was developed by the team of linguists developing the corpus. In the future, morpho-syntactic annotation of the texts collected in the corpus is also foreseen.

Notwithstanding the studies of adult foreigners' language, research of the language spoken by children and adolescents is very much required because at school we usually deal with a different educational perspective than in language courses (cf. Pospiszil-Hofmańska, Hofmański 2022). This is determined by the

---

6 The material of the latter two groups will constitute separate sub-corpora within 'FoKo'.
7 These are topics that are inherently close to the student, appealing to their experiences and emotions: 1. Bohater mojego życia [The hero of my life]; 2. Najszczęśliwszy dzień w moim życiu [Happiest day of my life]; 3. Szkoła przyszłości. [School of the Future.]
8 The transfer of the corpus to the TEITOK environment is currently under consideration.

specificity of the school[9] educational discourse covering a wide range of not only didactic but also educational activities and the diverse groups of its participants: teachers and other school staff as well as pupils and their parents[10]. In the most general terms, the linguistic situation of the subject of educational activities – the pupil – is significantly different from the situation of the students attending adult language courses or philology studies, who have achieved a sufficiently high competence in their mother tongue and are, by definition, strongly committed to working on improving their linguistic (and cultural) competence in Polish. The general linguistic development of a child is lower than that of an adult, and the goal of teaching Polish at school should be to equip the pupil with "linguistic competence to acquire knowledge and develop new study skills and to communicate effectively in school situations". Exploring formal language and the pupil's mastery of written language is also crucial." (Pamuła-Behrens 2018: 182).

As part of the collection of materials for the "FoKo" Corpus, one of the additional activities was to carry out a survey among teachers of Pomeranian educational institutions, the aim of which was to obtain information on the level of proficiency in Polish (in their subjective assessment)[11] among pupils with experience of migration in the family. Teachers were asked to determine to what extent the elements of the description of the 9 areas of language use apply to their pupils. These descriptive elements were of a more general nature, e.g. relating to attitudes towards speaking in Polish or the issue of mixing languages in a single utterance, and of a more specific nature when the elements concerned the degree of the development of particular language skills (listening, reading, speaking, writing). The surveyed teachers were given the option to tick one of 2 options to confirm the description: *true, rather true* , or 2 options to deny it: *rather untrue, untrue*. The survey results (percentages) based on 310 questionnaires have been presented in the table below:

---

9 By discourse, according to Anna Duszak's definition, I mean "the totality of a given act of communication, i.e. both the specific verbalisation (text) and the extra-linguistic factors that accompany it, i.e. above all the specific situation of use and its participants" (A. Duszak, 1989: 19).

10 Jolanta Nocoń considers as prototypical factors constituting this type of discourse: "(1) the characteristic sender-receiver interaction of the specialist-adept type (with the archetypal roles of teacher and student) and (2) the educational function, a specific communicative goal that can be defined as the aspiration of one of the parties (the teacher) to bring about a specific personality change in the interaction partner" (Nocoń 2020).

11 It is important to note here that the assessments made by the teachers do not represent the results of a reliable specialised diagnosis of language proficiency; they can only be a starting point for further research.

Area of linguistic action	True	Rather true	Rather untrue	Untrue
1. He speaks reluctantly	10.6	16	16.7	56.7
	26.6		73,4	
2. Has difficulty finding/selecting words	10	33	32.4	24.6
	43		57	
3. Has difficulty constructing sentences in speech	12.6	24.4	34.4	28.6
	37		63	
4. Has difficulty building sentences in writing	13.6	33.5	34.9	18
	47.1		52.9	
5. Has difficulty building longer spoken statements	18.4	30.9	29.9	20.8
	49,3		50.7	
6. Has difficulty building longer written statements	25.6	36.7	23.5	14.2
	62.3		37.7	
7. Does not understand what is being said to him/her	1	9,8	25.1	64.1
	10.8		89.2	
8. Cannot understand reading text	3	17.5	40.7	38.8
	20.5		79.5	
9. Mixes languages during one statement	12.4	19,5	27.2	40.9
	31.9		68.1	

Table 1. Level of Polish language proficiency among pupils with migration experience in the family studying in Pomeranian educational institutions in the years 2021–2023 (source: own survey based on materials collected in the "FoKo" Corpus).

The data in the table shows that the majority of the pupils surveyed feel that their teachers have quite well-developed receptive competences: they understand addressed oral speech (almost 90%) and do reasonably well with reading comprehension (almost 80%)[12]. Superimposing the information about the length of time that particular pupils have been residing in Poland on the survey data, it is also clear that these skills increase intensively as the student's immersion time in the Polish language environment increases. The majority of incoming foreign pupils start education with very limited knowledge of the Polish language (there were some who did not know enough Polish at the time of starting school to attend lessons at a Polish school at all), but very quickly develop receptive skills. These figures are not surprising given that the vast majority of pupils with current migration experience

---

12 The questionnaire did not specify which type of text was meant: written in general Polish or in a specialised language. However, as the questionnaire was completed mainly by Polish teachers, it can be assumed that these conclusions were based on an assessment of the reception of texts in formal language (additional comments included information that the student understands the instructions given in class) and literary language (understands the texts read in class).

are Slavic: those with Ukrainian or Russian as L1. These East Slavic languages, as well as the Belarusian language and mixed Russian-Ukrainian (Surzyk) and Russian-Belarusian (Trasyanka) varieties, although genetically do not belong to the closest relatives of West Slavic Polish, they show, however, great lexical and grammatical similarities resulting from centuries of contacts (cf. e.g. Kononenko 2012). The phenomenon of intercomprehension, i.e. understanding related languages without learning them first, has, undoubtedly, contributed to such good results in terms of students' understanding of Polish (cf. Doyé 2005: 60). This leads to the conclusion that it would be worthwhile to take conscious and targeted action to develop these intercomprehensive skills[13] both among foreign language learners (as a tool to facilitate and accelerate the acquisition of Polish as a foreign language) and among Polish-speaking learners as well as teachers and other school staff (as a tool to aid understanding of foreign language learners)[14]. This would be particularly valuable in a classroom setting where Polish-speaking students meet Ukrainian and/or Russian speakers – monolingual, bilingual and multilingual learners (often with different communicative habits and general experiences) who find themselves in a hitherto unfamiliar environment and linguistic landscape, and would also be in line with the contemporary perspective of considering the broad context of mastering more languages in education (Gębal 2016: 77). At the same time, one should also be aware that a foreign Slavic child is potentially in a better intercomprehensive situation, because he or she often (according to the surveys) knows two Slavic languages and is learning another one. The pupil sometimes also subconsciously projects the communicative ease he himself has achieved onto the teacher who, unfortunately, among the Slavic languages, usually only knows Polish and often does not even have basic information about the native language of his/her pupils.

In school communication, it is essential, as mentioned above, not only to use language for *strictly* educational purposes, but also for educational purposes, which requires nurturing a good relationship between teacher and student. As clinical and developmental research shows, these positive interpersonal relationships are particularly important for students in poor social, emotional and educational situations (Noam, Fiore, 2004: 9–14), and this is, after all, the sit-

---

13 Among the different levels of functioning of the term *intercomprehension* is also one that sees it as 'a pathway of specific didactic activities implemented as part of the language learning process' (Gębal 2016: 82). However, research is still needed on intercomprehension at the level of Slavic languages (cf. Saturno, Gębal 2022).

14 The intercomprehensive approach is based, firstly, on highlighting the similarities of the languages learnt, secondly, on raising awareness of the differences This involves referring to the existence of intemationalisms, a vocabulary common to the language family, the similarity of utterances, syntactic and morphosyntactic structures and word-formation rules (Gębal 2016: 83; Hofmański 2020).

uation which the majority of pupils with migrant experience attending Polish schools are in. To be effective, the communication between the teacher and the student should be a dialogue, take place in an atmosphere of acceptance, understanding and trust (Okon 2003: 51), and this requires, among other things, the ability to use language (including understanding one's interlocutor) in a way that is adapted not only to a given situation, but also to the needs of a particular student (Jagieła 2004). Interpersonal relationships between pupils (direct interactions or through different means of communication), especially those attending the same class, are also not insignificant for the quality of school communication. They, too, should be partners in a dialogues and attempt to understand their fellow interlocutor (in the most desirable way: without imposing the language of communication).

The language competences of the surveyed pupils with a migration experience are much worse in terms of productive skills: speaking and writing. According to the information provided by the teachers, pupils are mostly eager to speak, even though they lack vocabulary and mix languages relatively often in their statements. It is also very evident that pupils find it most difficult to produce written statements, especially longer ones (over 62% of pupils have such problems). However, it seems that the pupils' skill ratings given by the questionnaires are overestimated anyway, and in fact, the rating for productive skills (mainly writing) should be lower. For it is difficult to agree with the teacher's opinion that a boy from Russia from the 7th grade has no problems with constructing longer statements in writing, who presented his happiest day in life as follows: *Mój najszczęśliwszy dzień w moim życiu, To kiedy ja miałem urodziny. Ja z 3 swoimi kolegami poszedł do Jumpcity a Potem do kfc.* (63_M) or a first-year high school student who writes about the school of the future *Skołe przyszłości wyobrażam sobie jako miejsce gdzie dzieci będą zadowoleni z nauki orzaz nauczycieli. W przyszłej nauce będą stosowane komputery, dzieci by się uczyły z własnych zainteresowań. Nie będzie prac domowych oraz plan lekcij będzie wygodny tak jak dla uczniół ale też nauczycieli. Nauczycieli by mieli dobrą wypłate bo wykształcają przyszłe pokolenie.* (173_M).

There are, perhaps, several reasons for this. The aforementioned phenomenon of intercomprehension undoubtedly has a positive effect on the understanding of the message, but it no longer has such a positive effect on the productive competence[15], and may even have a negative effect on it in terms of the normativity of the message, as this type of approach to language teaching assumes a high tolerance for linguistic errors made by learners. A student who is understood by teachers and schoolmates may acquire the false belief that he or she is speaking

---

15 This does not mean that productive (oral and written) skills cannot be developed on the basis of acquired receptive skills (cf. Escudé, Janin 2010: 97).

correctly by transferring certain patterns, forms and structures from the native language into Polish (such as, in the example above *ja poszedl* [translator's note: taken directly from Russian, the correct Polish form would be *ja poszedlem*]).

Another reason can be found in the fact that, of the four skills of listening, reading, speaking and writing, the latter is generally the skill least used in people's everyday communicative activity. Although technological and civilizational changes and the intensive use of electronic media have forced modern language users to use writing, the forms of communication developed this way do not have the characteristics of the traditional written variety of language. As Jacek Warchala writes, 'the new media, preferring the image and the spoken word, are slowly destroying literacy under the influence of images, the sound form of the word, the situationality of the speech act, and are moving towards what I would call a patchwork way of thinking and formulating messages' (Warchala 278; cf. also. Skudrzyk 2005).

Writing is the only skill taught almost exclusively at school, primarily in the teaching of the mother tongue. In doing so, it requires very complex competences from the student. According to Agnieszka Rypel, these skills include not only the mere mastery of the writing technique (although in the case of Russian- and Ukrainian-speaking students an additional difficulty is writing in a different alphabet than in the native language, which is clearly confirmed by the materials collected in "FoKo"), but also: 1. overcoming the difficulties resulting from detachment from the particular speaking situation and from the lack of direct contact with the recipient; 2. mastering syntactic structures that are more complex than in the spoken language and show a high degree of stability; 3. using abstract vocabulary; 4. accordance to norms of correctness specific to the written variety; 5. mastering higher levels of text organisation; 6. using appropriate genre patterns; 7. using linguistic devices appropriate to the type of utterance and 8. applying the rules of spelling, punctuation and graphic organisation of the text (Rypel 2014: 311–312).

In school education, it is also important to note a certain asymmetry in the use of spoken and written language. Indeed, student written texts constitute a tool for diagnosing the degree and quality of mastering the learning content in various school subjects[16], even though new knowledge is mainly acquired by students through oral transmission (often the so-called transmission model – the student is the recipient of the knowledge given by the teacher). The formulation of statements in written language poses an additional problem for the learner, as he or she not only has to include relevant information in the statement (to present

---

16 This evaluative function is performed most extensively in Polish language lessons, where, as A. Rypel "measure themselves", i. e. they serve to check to what extent students have mastered specific textual skills' (Rypel 2014: 314).

his or her knowledge), but also to shape the statement accordingly. There is no support from the mother tongue, as even in this native language the relevant writing competence is most often still low and unestablished[17].

A low level of proficiency in the written variety of language (especially within its linguistic-stylistic component) is diagnosed in all students, not only those who struggle with the matter of a foreign language (cf. Guzy, Niesporek-Szamburska 2013). The student works collected in 'FoKo' are often very short (even limited to one sentence), and show the painstaking process of arriving at the final version of the text (numerous deletions and additions of both single letters and whole words and longer parts of speech, lexical changes and changes in word form, transformations within the syntax) not only in terms of determining the correct linguistic forms, but also in the search for appropriate means of expression. Compensating for the lack of ability to express thoughts and emotions is often done through the use of spelling habits specific to the language on the Internet (graphic characters).

Developing the ability to express oneself in written language (due to its dominant diagnostic and evaluative function in educational discourse) should be one of the priorities in schooling (cf. Pamuła-Behrens 2018: 182), although this will certainly not be an easy task. One would also postulate increased learner contact with written texts (working with subject textbooks), which is also characteristic of the aforementioned intercomprehensive approach in foreign language teaching (Gębal 2016: 86).

These activities would probably have to be combined with a general strengthening of foreign pupils' sense of the prestige and usefulness of Polish in acquiring knowledge. Indeed, teachers draw attention to the frequently low interest of children and young people with a migration experience in potentially mastering the Polish language to the best of their ability, stemming from the hope of returning to their homeland and to the former educational system. Low motivation to develop competences, especially in the area of productive language skills, manifests itself, according to the data contained in the questionnaires collected by "FoKo", in the mass use of various types of electronic communication support tools – from applications to online dictionaries and translators, reluctance to do homework (using the so-called "ready-made" materials) or frequent absences from additional Polish lessons.

Foreign pupils (as well as Polish students who started in a different education system), are often frustrated by the incompatibility of their language skills with the needs of school discourse. This is because relatively good fluency in everyday communication is accompanied by the lack of knowledge of specialist (dis-

---

17 According to many researchers, a good knowledge of the native language is needed to become highly competent in acquired languages.

cipline-related) vocabulary and the specific organisation of scientific texts. These students are unable to demonstrate their knowledge because they are unable to verbalise it. From the teacher's perspective, the pupil's evaluative work is also a kind of challenge – it requires an understanding of the message without being able to directly verify the correctness of this understanding and to separate the deficiencies resulting from an insufficient mastery of productive skills in a foreign language for the pupil from the lack of extra-linguistic knowledge.

Pupils are reluctant to take advantage of additional Polish language lessons, as the Polish they learn at the course is in fact neither the language of school education (a medium for acquiring new and expanding their existing knowledge and skills in various disciplines and subjects), nor the everyday language used by their peers – native speakers. On the one hand, thus, this manner and extent of language acquisition hardly facilitates the use of school aids and textbooks; on the other hand, the lack of a social dimension to the language taught at school (the variety is far from natural ways of communicating), makes it difficult to establish and build emotional bonds with peers speaking native Polish (Garncarek 2018: 20).

In order for additional Polish language lessons at school to be of adequate benefit, they should have a properly designed programme[18] aimed not only at developing the language of everyday communication, but also at supporting the learning of the language of school education (cf. Lewinska, Warda-Radys 2018). This variety of language has, in fact, its own characteristics, which include the official approach of the speakers, the high information load of the texts (brevity), abstract matters, the specific organisation of information, the choice of vocabulary (abstract words and specialist terminology), representational congruence and a low degree of message contextualisation (Seretny 2018: 143–144). Conscious development of the relevant competences within the language of school education is particularly important for pupils learning in a language that is foreign to them, as it is naturally the mother tongue that plays a significant role in cognition and ordering of the world (including the formation of consciousness and personality structure), making a person identify with it and usually think in it as an adult (Lipinska 2003: 15).

The juxtaposition of skills built on the syntactically and lexically simple Polish vocabulary learnt in Polish lessons as foreign language classes with the specialised language of school textbooks, the comprehension of which often poses difficulties even for Polish-speaking students (this comprehension cannot be done on a global level, but requires precision) can cause discouragement. Subsequently, this may have a negative impact on the intercompetitive level of

---

18 Ideally, the level of language should be diagnosed individually each time and a support system appropriate to the needs of the individual learner should be implemented.

comprehension in a foreign language, which depends not only on the student's degree of contact with the language in question, but also on attitudes towards it: ideas about its usefulness and a sense of its prestige (Dołowy-Rybińska 2021). It is, therefore, worth paying attention to, on the one hand, shaping positive attitudes of foreign language learners towards Polish and building confidence in their own cognitive abilities and, on the other hand, convincing them that passive knowledge of Polish alone is not enough to function well in Poland.

Intercomprehensive solutions, which constitute a natural way of rapidly assimilating similar language systems, should prove effective for the rapid adaptation of foreign-language pupils to the Polish educational system and equip them with the linguistic competence to acquire knowledge in Polish. Once pupils have reached a higher level of language, measures can be taken to eliminate interference errors from their language. The intercomprehensive approach should also be an opportunity for other participants in the educational discourse to establish an understanding with pupils with a migrant experience.

It is also important to emphasize the educational value of intercomprehension not only as an effective tool to promote understanding in a school communication situation, but also to facilitate adaptation and integration processes. Indeed, it fosters intercultural awareness (by not imposing an external language) in communication, allowing for a better and deeper understanding of difference and respect for the cultural specificities of others, including foreign language (Capucho 2012).

Bibliography

Arabski J., 1996, *Przyswajanie języka obcego i pamięci werbalnej*, Katowice.

Capucho M.F., 2012, *Intercomprehension – language tools for intercultural communication.* "Redefining Community in Intercultural Context" 1, p. 9–18.

Dołowy-Rybińska N., 2021, *Interkomprehensja języków słowiańskich jako czynnik motywujący do nauki języka górnołużyckiego dla uczniów Gimnazjum Górnołużyckiego pochodzi z niemieckojęzycznych rodzin*, "Zeszyty Łużyckie", 55, p. 299–318. https://doi.org/10.32798/zl.812.

Doyé P., 2005, *Intercomprehension. Guide for the development of language education policies in Europe: from linguistic diversity to plurilingual education.* Reference study. Retrieved from Council of Europe, Language Policy Division: https://www.coe.int/t/dg 4/linguistic/Source/Doye%20EN.pdf.

Duszak A., 1989, *Tekst, dyskurs, komunikacja międzykulturowa*, Warszawa 1989.

Escudé P., Janin P., 2010, *L'intercompréhension, clé du plurilinguisme, clé international*, Paris.

Garncarek P., 2018, *Nauczanie dzieci języków obcych w kontekście akwizycji pierwszego języka*, "Postscriptum Polonistyczne" 2, p. 13–24; doi: 10.31261/PS_P.2018.22.01.

Guzy A., Niesporek-Szamburska U., 2013, *Uczniowskie zinterkomprehensymagania ze słowem. O pisaniu dłuższej formy wypowiedzi na różnych poziomach nauczania*, "Annales Universitatis Paedagogicae Cracoviensis. Studia ad Didacticam Litterarum Polonarum et Linguae Polonae Pertinentia" IV, p. 45–63.

Gębal P., 2016, *Interkomprehensja, strategie mediacyjne i nauczanie języków obcych*, [w:] Tłumaczenie dydaktyczne w nowoczesnym kształceniu językowym: monografia zbiorowa pod red. E. Lipińskiej. A. Seretny, Kraków: Księgarnia Akademicka, p. 77–93.

Hofmański W., 2020, *Jak (z)rozumieć obcy język pokrewny? Słowiańska adaptacja "techniki siedmiu sit" (na materiale czesko-polskim)*, "Socjolingwistyka" XXXIV, p. 215–230; http://dx.doi.org/10.17651/SOCJOLING.34.13.

Jagieła J., 2004, *Komunikacja w szkole. Krótki poradnik psychologiczny*. Kraków.

Kononenko I., 2012, *Język ukraiński i polski: studium kontrastywne*, Warszawa (Wyd. UW).

Lewińska A., Warda-Radys L., 2018, *Nauczanie języka polskiego jako obcego/drugiego a sukces edukacyjny ucznia z doświadczeniem migracyjnym (na przykładzie pracy nad leksyką)*, [w:] *Edukacja wobec migracji. Konteksty glottodydaktyczne i pedagogiczne. Monografia zbiorowa*, red. P. Gębal, Księgarnia Akademicka, Kraków, p. 103–116.

Lipińska E., Seretny A., 2012, *Między językiem ojczystym a obcym. Nauczanie i uczenie się języka odziedziczonego na przykładzie chicagowskiej diaspory polonijnej*. Kraków.

Lipińska E., 2003, *Język ojczysty, język obcy, język drugi: wstęp do badań dwujęzyczności*, Kraków: Wydawnictwo Uniwersytetu Jagiellońskiego.

Noam G. G., Fiore N., 2004, *Relationships across multiple settings: An overview*. "New Directions for Youth Development" 103, p. 9–16.

Nocoń J., 2020, *Stylistyczne aspekty dyskursu edukacyjnego*, [w:] Odmiany stylowe polszczyzny dawniej i dziś, red. U. Sokólska, Białystok 2011, p. 187–200.

Okoń W., 2003, *Komunikacja interpersonalna w szkole*. "Edukacja i Dialog" 1, p. 50–53.

Pamuła-Behrens M., 2018, *Język edukacji szkolnej w integracyjnym modelu wsparcia ucznia z doświadczeniem migracji w rodzinie*, "Postscriptum Polonistyczne", 2 (22), p. 171–186; doi: 10.31261/PS_P.2018.22.11.

Pospiszil-Hofmańska K., i Hofmański W., 2022, *Interkomprehensja – interferencja – integracja. Polszczyzna w perspektywie nauczania użytkowników języków wschodniosłowiańskich*, "Poznańskie Studia Slawistyczne", p. 253–271.

Rittel T., 1992, *Model analityczny języka w komunikacji szkolnej (ujęcie lingwoedukacyjne)*, "Rocznik Naukowo-Dydaktyczny WSP. Prace Językoznawcze" VII, p. 123–138.

Rypel A., 2014, *Język pisany w szkole – między kreatywnością a schematem*; [w:] *Językowe, literackie i kulturowe ścieżki edukacji polonistycznej (tradycja i współczesność): księga jubileuszowa dedykowana profesor Helenie Synowiec w czterdziestolecie pracy naukowej i dydaktycznej*, red. D. Krzyżyk, B. Niesporek-Szamburska., p. 311–321.

Saturno J., Gębal P., 2022, *Interkomprehensja w nauczaniu języka polskiego jako obcego (jpjo) słowian wschodnich*, "Acta Universitatis Lodziensis. Kształcenie Polonistyczne Cudzoziemców" 29, p. 213–229; https://doi.org/10.18778/0860-6587.29.14.

Seretny A., 2018, *Język szkolnej edukacji w perspektywie glottodydaktycznej – zarys problematyki*; "Postsciptum Polonistyczne" 2, p. 139–156; doi: 10.31261/PS_P.2018.22.09.

Skudrzyk A., 2005, *Czy zmierzch kultury pisma? O synestezji i analfabetyzmie funkcjonalnym*, Katowice.

Warchala J., 2020, *Piśmienność i oralność, czyli język w czasach cyfryzacji*, [w:] Polszczyzna w dobie cyfryzacji, red. A. Hącia, K. Kłosińska i P. Zbróg, p. 277–288.

Part Three.
New Developments: Woman perspective – Everyday practice –
Netnolinguistics

Dominika Izdebska-Długosz (Jagiellonian University Kraków)

Ukrainian refugee women in Poland – Determinants of Polish language acquisition two years after the outbreak of the war

Abstract

The article discusses the results of research into female Ukrainian war refugees regarding their knowledge of the Polish language, plans related to learning, undertaking or abstaining from learning Polish, as well as factors facilitating or hindering it. The article primarily focuses on the results of the latest measurement from October/November 2023, that is, 19 months after the outbreak of the war in Ukraine. At certain points, comparisons to the previous measurement from April/May 2022 are made. These comparisons allow for observing the changes that have occurred in the lives of refugee women regarding the studied issues over these months.

Introduction

It has been two years since Russia invaded Ukraine on 24 February 2024. The war that erupted beyond Poland's eastern border has resulted in a massive and unprecedented influx of refugees from Ukraine to Poland. Due to the necessity for men to remain in Ukraine, mainly women have arrived in Poland.

In our previous collective research on Ukrainian refugees in Poland, which will be referenced throughout this paper, conducted in April/May 2022 on a sample of 737 war refugees from Ukraine residing in Poland, it was revealed that, due to the military conflict, 97% of the refugees who arrived in Poland were female, with only 3% being male. The average age was 37 years, and ¾ of the refugees arrived with children (Długosz, Kryvachuk, Izdebska-Długosz 2022: 6).

In the subsequent measurement carried out in October/November 2023, 19 months after the Russian invasion, only women, that is, female Ukrainian war refugees were examined. The aim of the subsequent measurement was to determine the changes and their determinants in the following areas:

1. Socio-demographic characteristics (age, education, place of residence before the outbreak of the war, financial situation before the war, family situation, marital status, number and age of children)
2. Children's education

3. Knowledge of the Polish language
4. Living conditions in Poland
5. Quality of life in the current place of residence (trust, satisfaction with living conditions, relations with local population, temperature of mutual relations, change in Poles' attitudes towards refugees, adaptation problems of refugee children)
6. Mobility
7. Employment
8. Social practices in the place of residence
9. Mental health
10. Plans for the future   (Długosz & Izdebska-Długosz 2024)

This article explores issues related to the knowledge of the Polish language among refugees, the learning process, and its determinants. The results obtained in the current research will be compared with those obtained almost two years ago.

1.   Ukrainian-speaking individuals and the Polish language

The absolutely fundamental issues related to the acquisition and learning of the Polish language in the Ukrainian-speaking environment need to be outlined.

The specificity of the glottodidactic system, in which Ukrainians learning Polish as a foreign language find themselves, primarily arises from a linguistic-cultural encounter between two similar Slavic qualities: Ukrainian and Polish. In linguistic terms, we are dealing with languages from the East Slavic (Ukrainian) and West Slavic (Polish) groups. These languages are similar – both are inflected languages with the same number of cases in declension, possess identical grammatical categories (although they are realized differently, such as e.g. grammatical gender), have similar syntax, and share up to 70% of vocabulary (*Які європейські мови найближчі між собою*. https://gazeta.ua/articles/istoriya -movi/_aki-yevropejski-movi-najblizhchi-mizh-soboyu/701681 [accessed: 1 October 2021]). From the similarity between the languages in the process of acquisition and learning, two phenomena emerge, which shape both the pace of learning and acquisition of Polish by this group of learners, as well as the quality of their Polish-Ukrainian interlanguage[1].

---

1 In this paper, *interlanguage* is understood as an *approximative system*, according to William Nemser's definition. It is "a system deviating from the norm, currently used by the learner who attempts to use the target language. Such approximative systems vary depending on the degree of proficiency" (Arabski 1979: 10).

The first phenomenon is *negative transfer* (*interference*)[2], which involves transposition of what is known from the source language (first language – further referred to as L1) onto new linguistic material (second language – further referred to as L2). In the case of Ukrainians, we usually speak of Ukrainian-Russian bilingualism[3], therefore, elements from both of these languages (perceived as a broader single L1), such as inflectional suffixes, derivational morphemes, inflectional paradigms, ways of realizing individual grammatical categories, syntactic structures (calques) are transferred to the Polish language spoken by Ukrainians, and consequently to their Polish-Ukrainian interlanguage (Izdebska-Długosz 2021; Krawczuk 2005, 2007, 2011 et al.; Kowalewski 2017; Zielińska 2018). The transposition of linguistic elements manifests itself in the interlanguage in the form of language errors. Therefore, the more similar the languages are, the stronger the interference will be – the stronger and more longlasting the process of transferring linguistic elements from L1 to L2, and more errors will appear in language production; however, reception is not free of these errors either.

Negative transfer, or rather its empirical traces in interlanguage, namely language errors, is currently a well-researched topic (for references on the subject matter – see: Izdebska-Długosz 2021: 91–96). Difficulties have been defined and presented in a number of written works, both detailed and monographic (error corpora).

The situation is different in the case of the second phenomenon that affects the Polish language spoken by Ukrainians, which requires further research. This phenomenon is *intercomprehension*, which is the ability to understand a language without prior learning. Such a possibility arises mainly in the case of very similar language systems, largely based on similar vocabulary (an example of this may be the mutual understanding between Poles and Slovaks, and to a lesser extent between Poles and Czechs). The prerequisite for understanding is, of course, hearing the acoustic image of the sign (in accordance with the structure of the linguistic sign), which is why learning to read is so important.

---

2 *Negative transfer*, also known as *interference*, in psychological terms, refers to the negative impact of fully automated habits of the primary language on the still developing habits in L2. It also involves the perception, storage, and reproduction of foreign elements in the form of L1. In linguistic terms, interference is the overlapping (crossing, mixing) of systems of different languages, resulting in the use of elements of one language system in the other. In terms of glottodidactics, it is a part of the process of acquiring a foreign language, in which the learner is the subject. It is also a factor causing a particular type of error made by the learner under the influence of habits and structures of L1 (Magnuszewska 1981: 14; Iwan 1995: 39–40).

3 This phenomenon even applies to trilingualism (Lewczuk 2020). It is also necessary to take into account the changing statuses of the Ukrainian and Russian languages prompted by the war with Russia, as well as fluctuation in Ukrainians' attitudes towards their own bilingualism (Yaremko, Levchuk 2023; Levchuk 2023).

Intercomprehension among Ukrainian learners of Polish is a phenomenon described less extensively than interference; nonetheless, many researchers currently lean towards recognizing the possibility of utilizing positive transfer in teaching Polish in the Ukrainian-speaking environment (Jasińska 2013; Gębal 2016; Gębal & Saturno 2022).

The aforementioned phenomena affect language skills in such a way that receptive skills are almost inherently higher in Ukrainian-speaking individuals than in groups using other L1s, while productive skills may suffer in quality due to an excess of language inaccuracies, which may require more time for improvement and combating transfer errors. This creates a characteristic gap between the two groups of language skills, which cannot be overlooked in teaching Polish to Ukrainians.

2. Research methodology

The results presented in this text, which pertain to issues related to the knowledge of the Polish language and its learning among Ukrainian refugee women, are part of – as mentioned earlier – a larger quantitative study conducted on a sample of 466 individuals. It was carried out using an online CAWI (Computer-Assisted Web Interview) survey in October and November 2023. The sample for the study was selected based on the availability of respondents. The questionnaire in Ukrainian was created using LimeSurvey, a free online survey tool, and distributed through various on-line channels (Długosz & Izdebska-Długosz 2024:...).

The quantitative study was analysed using the SPSS statistical software.

3. Female Ukrainian war refugees and the Polish language

Part of a larger study on female Ukrainian war refugees, described in the monograph (Długosz & Izdebska-Długosz 2024), concerns the knowledge of the Polish language and various related determinants[4].

The knowledge of the language of the host country is crucial for the adaptation and further integration processes experienced by immigrants, including refugees. Mastering the language and cultural scripts are key cultural competencies of immigrants (Heckmann 2006 cited in: Brzozowska 2022: 58). Acquiring the

---

4 The monograph presents the determinants of the main phenomena related to Polish spoken by Ukrainian refugee women, which are discussed in this paper. These conditions were identified by means of statistical correlation analysis. Due to the parametric limitations of the article, their presentation has been omitted.

language of the host country is not only a fundamental indicator of immigrants' integration in the cultural dimension, but it also determines their position and opportunities in the labor market and their interactions with the local population. It allows them to seek employment in line with their education and skills acquired in their home country; it enables them to settle in a foreign country and live decently, and the said country and new society cease to be foreign; it allows for full participation in social life in the host country.

Therefore, it becomes evident that the issues of language acquisition and learning by war refugees are always within the scope of interest of researchers from the field of migration sociology (Brzozowska 2022; Pindel 2014), rather than solely researchers in glottodidactics, who interested in the processes of acquiring a foreign language by a specific group using a particular L1. In this paper, the aim was to combine both of these approaches: the sociological-migratory perspective and the glottodidactic and linguistic perspective.

3.1. Declared level of proficiency in Polish

To examine the declared level of proficiency in the Polish language, a semi-open question was used, with a set of available responses containing appropriately operationalised levels of proficiency in Polish.

The chart allows for the observation changes that occurred between April/May 2022 and October/November 2023.

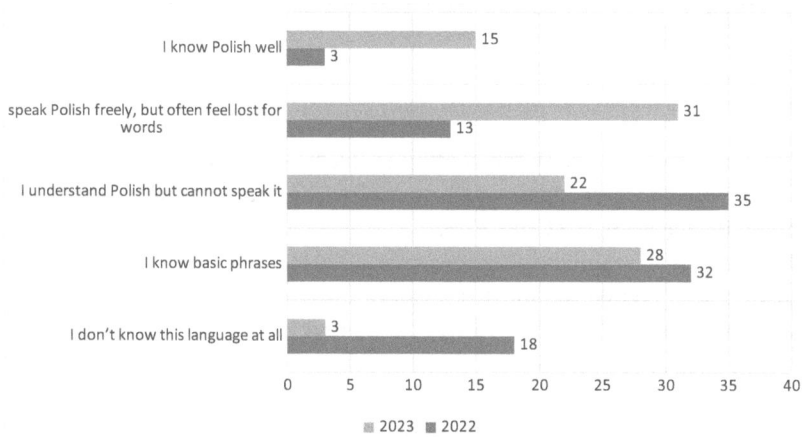

Chart 1. Declared level of proficiency in Polish. Source: own research

The chart shows significant changes in the declared level of proficiency in the Polish language among female Ukrainian refugees. There was an inversely proportional change among those who had the poorest and the best knowledge of Polish: the percentage of the former decreased from 18% to 3%, while the percentage of the latter increased from 3% to 15%. There was a slight decrease in the percentage of those who only know basic phrases (from 32% to 28%), and a significant increase of those who speak Polish, but experience lexical gaps (from 13% to 31%).

This shift in language proficiency from weaker to stronger is even more pronounced on the radar chart.

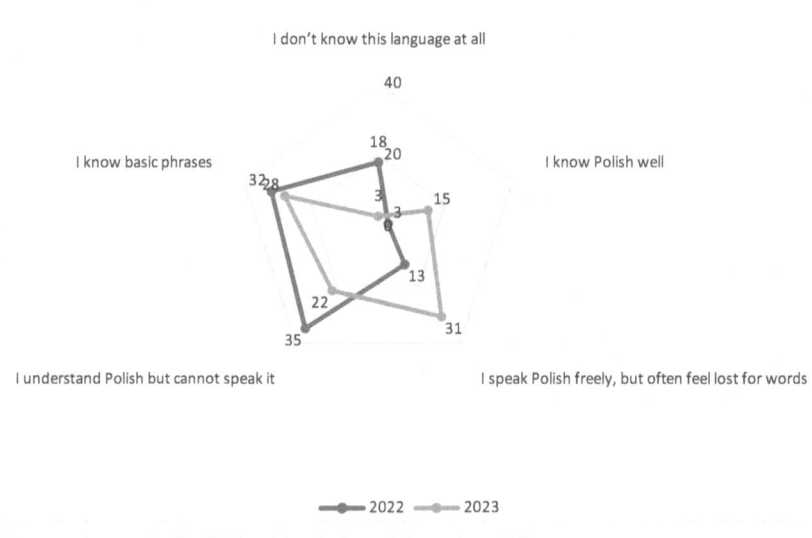

Chart 2. Changes in the declared level of proficiency in Polish 2022–2023. Source: own research

It is evident how the area on the continuum from the weakest to the strongest proficiency in Polish changes, which is marked by the percentage points appropriate for the years 2022 and 2023.

Undoubtedly, Ukrainian refugee women in 2023 already had a better command of Polish. While the most frequently selected response in 2022 was "I understand Polish but cannot speak it" (35%), now it is the item "I speak Polish freely, but often feel lost for words" (31%). This could be rather loosely defined as a transition from level A1-A2 to B1-B2. However, it is certainly not the time to celebrate success. It is beyond any doubt that the proficiency in Polish of the respondents requires further improvement, especially in the context of educational and professional life in Poland.

3.2. Undertaking Polish language learning

An important consideration is whether the respondents embarked on planned learning of Polish upon arriving in Poland. The vast majority of respondents confirmed undertaking Polish language learning.

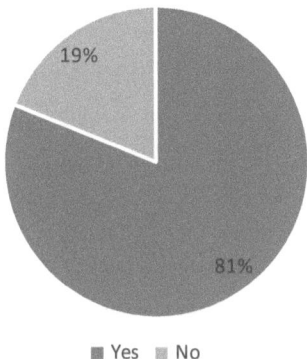

19%

81%

■ Yes ■ No

Chart 3. Undertaking Polish language learning upon arrival in Poland (in %). Source: own research

This fact is not surprising, especially in the context of the numerous free "survival" Polish language courses organized for refugees at that time – short, intensive courses allowing for immersion in the language, getting acquainted with its structure, familiarizing with differences and similarities, as compared to the refugees' L1. Above all, the courses aimed to equip the refugees with the ability to read, thus enabling the mechanism of intercomprehension.

3.3. Forms of learning Polish as a foreign language

Another important issue is the type of course attended by the respondents – what was the form of planned learning of the Polish language. Refugees were asked the same question in 2022, therefore, the same question could be used in the new measurement in order to examine any changes in this matter.

As shown, the most popular response in the first measurement in 2022 was self-study of the language, which in fact could mean the lack thereof (and/or contact with language material through conversations with Poles, films, songs, the Internet, etc.) – this was as high as 69% at the time. Currently – in the 2023 measurement – it is the second most frequently selected response (27%), with the most popular being courses organized by foundations and associations.

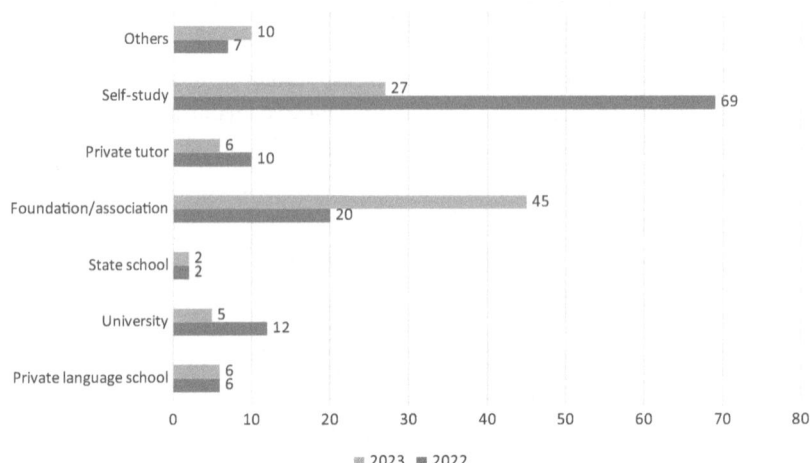

Chart 4. Forms of learning Polish. Source: own research

The necessity of even basic adaptation in a new place, a period of chaos and stress among refugees, certainly did not facilitate undertaking Polish language learning immediately upon their arrival in Poland.

Some respondents participated in free courses organized by higher education institutions, and currently this percentage has decreased (from 12% to 5%), which is not surprising, as universities now almost no longer have free courses in their offer. Refugees have been living in Poland long enough to be able to find attractive course offers for themselves – this is evidenced by the popularity of aid programmes offered by various foundations and associations – such courses are currently chosen by as many as 45% of respondents.

Fewer respondents are currently undertaking learning with a private tutor (a decrease from 10% to 6%). Courses organized by Polish state schools and language schools (presumably payable) remain at the same level.

Some individuals (10%) selected the option "other", mentioning the following types of courses: in a church in Warsaw; courses for teachers (Teacher Training Centre in Krakow); initially self-study, then in a post-secondary school; learning in Ukraine before coming to Poland (language courses for workplace purposes); courses organized by the Polish Labour Office; learning with a volunteer tutor; courses organized by UNICEF; through participation in projects; thanks to working with their own children.

3.4.　Duration of Polish language learning

An important issue is the duration of Polish language learning – whether refugee women have already completed this process, how long it lasted, or whether it is still continued.

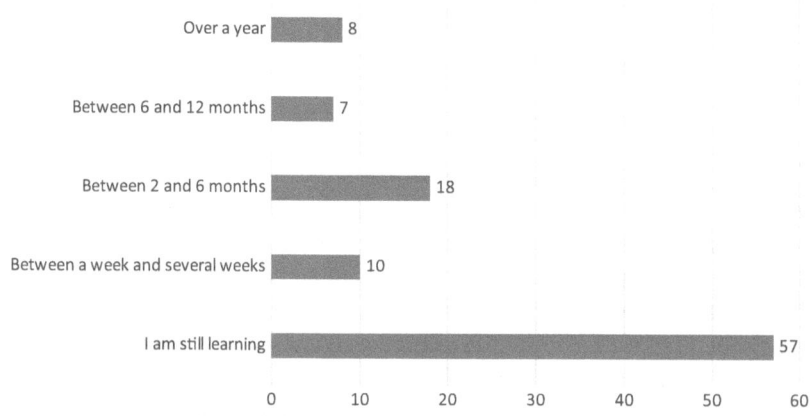

Chart 5. Duration of Polish language learning. Source: own research

More than half of the refugees are still learning Polish – thus, the process of mastering the language continues, which shall be considered a reasonable undertaking. The remaining respondents are not currently learning the language. The shortest duration of learning Polish was reported by 10% of the respondents. Courses which were a few months long turned out to be more popular (18%) than the ones of longer duration (a total of 15%).

3.5.　Motivation behind not undertaking Polish language learning

The respondents answered an open-ended question, the purpose of which was to determine the reasons why they did not engage in Polish language learning. It's worth noting that 19% of the respondents belong in this category (see Chart 3).
　The obtained responses indicate various types of "shortcomings":
– lack of time (due to the need to seek/undertake employment, attend to existential matters);
– lack of necessity (similarities between languages, prior knowledge of Polish, frequent contacts with Poles that suffice);
– lack of motivation;
– lack of financial means for paid courses and no access to free courses;

- lack of a good teacher;
- lack of contact with Poles – contacting only Ukrainians;
- due to the necessity of assisting their children in learning (learning through this method);
- having young children, no possibility of leaving them with a caretaker, the need to take care of them;
- belief that the war will end quickly and there will be an opportunity to return home quickly;
- difficult material;
- health issues.

The most frequent responses concerned the women's existential issues, as they are busy caring for young children or working. Such life situations result in a lack of time, opportunities, energy, or financial resources. Free language courses were offered massively to refugees in the spring and summer months of 2022. Currently, most courses are payable – especially considering the fact that courses at higher levels of proficiency are already needed. It is also worth noting that the vast majority of female refugees have children and came to Poland without a spouse. Thus, the responsibility to provide care for their children falls on them, both at home, at school, and also in financial terms.

Lack of motivation – which also appeared in the responses – was most often associated with the belief that the war would soon end, and if one does not intend to stay in Poland, then there is no point in investing time, financial resources, and effort in learning the language. It is difficult to find the strength to learn a new language when one is anxiously waiting to return home.

Some respondents did not understand that the question pertained to not undertaking language learning after arriving in Poland, following the outbreak of the war with Russia, and responded that there was no such need before the war, nor did they have any plans related to a prospective stay in Poland. This also demonstrates that we are dealing with forced, unplanned migration, with exile – such a situation certainly does not facilitate the desire to learn a foreign language.

In the first survey in 2022, respondents were also asked why they did not intend to learn Polish (at that time, 81% planned to learn Polish, 4% did not intend to, and 15% expressed uncertainty – Izdebska-Długosz 2022: 219). In 2022, as many as 47% indicated the desire for a quick return to Ukraine as the main reason (Izdebska-Długosz 2022: 222). We may expect that some of these individuals have returned to Ukraine. Perhaps they had more difficulty adapting to Polish conditions.

Today, the expectation of returning home is a motivation that appears in responses marginally. Unfortunately, these hopes for a quick return have failed, as the war continues, and no one knows when it might end. Refugee women living in Poland are already "settled", and it is day-to-day existential matters that prevent or hinder their language learning. Therefore, the internal motivations have turned into external ones. This is evidenced by other responses selected in the first measurement: 20% of respondents selected the answer "I have other things on my mind now", and 18% could not find free courses. Therefore, it is evident how much has changed during these 19 months between the first and the second measurement. From almost "sitting on suitcases", waiting for a signal to return home, the refugees transitioned to women who are well-integrated with the Polish system, life, and society, and who are busy with work and home life.

3.6. Factors facilitating and hindering the learning of the Polish language

In the subsequent open-ended question, the refugee women were asked what helped them learn Polish, and what was the hindering factor, impeding the learning process.

Among the dominant factors that facilitated the learning of the Polish language were primarily free language courses attended by the respondents, discussion clubs offering language practice, good tutors (native speakers of Polish, which was emphasized), good coursebooks, and teaching aids.

Frequent contacts with Poles turned out to be yet another factor. These contacts were taking place primarily at work, at the children's school/kindergarten, in shops, at the doctor's. Additionally, the desire to meet new Polish-speaking friends, the need to immerse oneself in a Polish-speaking environment through social interactions, and thus becoming rooted in it, were also mentioned.

Linguistic benefits arising from the necessity of helping children with their education, during which the mother also learns, were also mentioned. Living in a Polish-speaking environment, thus the language acquisition *per se*, as well as reading magazines and books, browsing the Internet websites in Polish, watching Polish TV, and listening to the radio – thus constant exposure to linguistic input – was also significant. Temporary stays with Polish families also helped, which – as known – was a common solution to housing issues for refugees right after the outbreak of the war in Ukraine. The warm reception of immigrant women by Poles was also highlighted, along with the cordial attitude towards them, which had a positive impact on their willingness to learn the language.

Personal motivation and perseverance also proved important; the awareness of the necessity to learn the language in order to find employment, support their children, and live in a foreign country. Language aptitude or curiosity about the new Polish culture were also significant for some of the respondents. Lastly, the similarity and proximity of the Polish language to the Ukrainian language also facilitated the process of learning Polish.

Despite focusing on many positive determinants for learning and acquiring Polish, more attention was often paid to hindrances connected with the possibilities of learning Polish. The factors hindering the learning process are identical to those preventing the undertaking of language learning for 19% of respondents from the previous question.

This is most often due to a lack of time, associated with both the necessity of working to support children in Poland and taking care of younger children, the inability to leave them with a caretaker during study time.

Yet another factor hindering the learning process turned out to be a lack of financial means. While courses offered in Poland immediately after the outbreak of the war were free of charge, for those at higher levels of proficiency (from A2 upwards), payment is usually required. This constitutes a barrier to language improvement for female refugees. Free courses were too short – the Ukrainians also mention this issue.

There is also mention of a lack of strength to undertake learning; a lack of a suitable tutor (who would correct linguistic errors), a lack of contracts with Poles (this presumably concerns mainly unemployed women who take care of their children at home).

Respondents also mention difficulties related to the matter of the Polish language *per se:* the Polish language is difficult (and courses are too intensive, it is difficult to remember everything), it is difficult to write correctly, compose sentences, remember new lexical items, and speak. There are not enough grammar exercises in courses. Polish cannot be learned entirely independently, without professional help: "It's hard to learn on your own. It seems like you understand everything, but it's hard to speak out".

The fact that the desire for a quick return to Ukraine did not help in learning the new language was also stressed. A certain psychological barrier in a situation where departure from the homeland was not planned but was forced upon them was also mentioned. One of the respondents expressed this issue as follows: "our thoughts were racing home".

As shown, the same factors that hinder effective learning of the Polish language were also mentioned as those preventing it.

It is difficult to change the lives of female refugees related to the necessity of earning a living and taking care of children. Nevertheless, it is definitely possible and worth taking steps that could help them improve their language skills. This question is addressed in the final subsection of this article.

4.   Glottodidactic implications and beyond

In 2022, while describing the first study into Ukrainian refugee women in an article, I stated in the conclusion that time would slowly come for further language improvement, after the wave of intensive survival courses. Therefore, the language offer for Ukrainians must follow this need (Izdebska-Długosz 2022: 223–224). These opinions are confirmed in the new measurement – especially in the factors preventing and/or hindering the learning Polish as a foreign language.

In addition to daily life issues, such as the need to work, childcare, the lack of time or strength, the lack of free courses at higher language proficiency levels is mentioned equally frequently. It seems that the first need at this moment is to provide refugees with access to free (as many aid programs are currently carried out, including those funded by EU funds) Polish language courses at higher proficiency levels, but above all, focused on their vocational language education – teaching specialist languages (medical language, legal language, metalanguages of individual school subjects for female teachers) in order to enable refugees to achieve full personal and professional development, fulfil their professional aspirations, and thus enrich the Polish labour market with highly qualified, disciplined, and self-motivated employees.

A place where such courses take place, offering also temporary childcare for refugees in the form of animation while their mothers learn Polish, would be a perfect solution, allowing many of the female refugees to participate in such courses. It also seems that a good solution would be to limit classical homework assignments in favor of listening and reading materials related to specific professional activities.

While teaching Polish to female Ukrainian refugees, awareness of the effects of interference on the one hand and intercomprehension on the other is required. One should consider avoiding the effects of negative transfer, while simultaneously skillfully utilizing the advantage of positive transfer.

Nowadays, we are dealing with a dynamic and integrating group of Ukrainian women who, after a period of initial adaptation and settling in Poland, want more – to work in their learned professions, use the qualifications and competencies acquired in Ukraine, and also pursue their aspirations (Długosz & Izdebska-Długosz 2024), undoubtedly the key to which is mastering the Polish language.

Bibliography

Arabski, Janusz. 1979. *Errors as indications of the development of interlanguage*. Katowice: Uniwersytet Śląski.

Brzozowska, Anita. 2022. *Przez szklany próg. Integracja i mobilność społeczno-ekonomiczna z Ukrainy zawierających małżeństwa z obywatelami Polski*. Warszawa: Wydawnictwa Uniwersytetu Warszawskiego.

Długosz, Piotr & Izdebska-Długosz, Dominika. 2024. *Uchodźczynie wojenne z Ukrainy: dwa lata od inwazji*. Lublin: Academicon.

Długosz, Piotr & Kryvachuk, Liudmyla & Izdebska-Długosz, Dominika. 2022. *Uchodźcy wojenni z Ukrainy. Życie w Polsce i plany na przyszłość*. Kraków: Academicon.

Gębal, Przemysław & Saturno, Jacopo. 2022. Interkomprehensja w nauczaniu języka polskiego jako obcego (JPJO) Słowian wschodnich. *Acta Universitatis Lodzensis. Kształcenie Polonistyczne Cudzoziemców* 29, 213–229.

Gębal, Przemysław E. 2016. Interkomprehensja, strategie mediacyjne i nauczanie języków obcych. In E. Lipińska, A. Seretny (ed), *Tłumaczenie dydaktyczne w nowoczesnym nauczaniu językowym*, 77–93. Kraków: Universitas.

Iwan, Katarzyna. 1995. *Działanie transferu międzyjęzykowego w zakresie opanowania ortografii rosyjskiej w środowisku polskojęzycznym*. Szczecin: Wydawnictwo Naukowe Uniwersytetu Szczecińskiego.

Izdebska-Długosz, Dominika. 2021. *Błędy gramatyczne w polszczyźnie studentów ukraińskojęzycznych*. Kraków: Księgarnia Akademicka.

Izdebska-Długosz, Dominika. 2022. Uchodźcy z Ukrainy w Polsce – znajomość polszczyzny, plany na przyszłość, nauka języka. In S. Butko, M. Gębka-Wolak (ed.), *Polsko-ukraińskie spotkania językowe*, 213–226. Toruń: Wydawnictwo Naukowe Uniwersytetu Mikołaja Kopernika.

Jaki jevropejski movy najblyžči miž soboju. (Які європейські мови найближчі між собою). (https://gazeta.ua/articles/istoriya-movi/_aki-yevropejski-movi-najblizhchi-mizh-sob oyu/701681) (Accessed 2021–10–01).

Jasińska, Agnieszka. 2013. O interkomprehensji w nauczaniu języka polskiego jako obcego. *Polski w Niemczech. Pismo Federalnego Związku Nauczycieli Języka Polskiego* 1, 68–75.

Kowalewski, Jerzy. 2017. *Język polski na Ukrainie w perspektywie glottodydaktycznej*. Kraków.

Krawczuk, Ałła. 2005. Trudne miejsca w gramatyce polskiej dla Ukraińców (w związku z przygotowywaniem podręcznika "Polska fleksja z ćwiczeniami dla Ukraińców"). In P. Garncarek (ed.), *Nauczanie języka polskiego jako obcego i polskiej kultury w nowej rzeczywistości europejskiej*, 491–497. Warszawa: Uniwersytet Warszawski.

Krawczuk, Ałła. 2007. Błędy gramatyczne studentów polonistyki lwowskiej powodowane polsko-ukraińską interferencją. In M. Czermińska. K. Meller. P. Fliciński (ed.), *Literatura, kultura i język polski w kontekstach i kontaktach światowych*, 809–823. Poznań: Wydawnictwo Naukowe UAM.

Krawczuk, Ałła. 2011. Błędy językowe w polszczyźnie Ukraińców powodujące zakłócenia komunikacji z Polakami. In I. Masojć, H. Sokołowska (ed.), *Tożsamość na styku kultur*, 480–494. Vilnius: Edukologija.

Lewczuk, Paweł. 2020. *Trójjęzyczność ukraińsko-rosyjsko-polska Ukraińców niepolskiego pochodzenia.* Kraków: Księgarnia Akademicka.

Magnuszewska, Zofia. 1981. *O błędach językowych spowodowanych interferencją (na przykładzie analizy systemu morfosyntaktycznego i leksykalnego języka francuskiego).* Zielona Góra: Wyższa Szkoła Pedagogiczna.

Paweł, Levchuk. 2023. *Rosijska mova ma ukraintsi: ščo zminylosja u 2023 roci?* (Російська мова та українці: що змінилося у 2023 році?), (https://lb.ua/blog/pavlo_levchuk/582 940_rosiyska_mova_ukraintsi_shcho.html?fbclid=IwAR1vFN3CrPK7tdQb9EY2ABb41 GeH7-0dY-PtEAyH6ZP-DltbmZM4_BZmQko) (Accessed 2024-11-02.)

Pindel, Edyta. (ed.). 2014. *Imigranci w Małopolsce. Między integracją, asymilacją, separacją, marginalizacją.* Kraków: Akademia Ignatianum w Krakowie.

Yaremko, Liliya & Levchuk, Paweł. 2023. Language Consciousness and Ukrainian Students' Attitudes Towards the Ukrainian Language in a Time of War. *Cognitive Studies | Études cognitives* No 23.

Zelinska, Marija. (Зелінська, Марія) 2018. *Komunikativna kompetencja molodyh nosijiv polskoj movy zahidnyh oblastiej Ukrajiny* (Комунікативна компетенція молодих носіїв польської мови західних областей України). Drohobycz: ПП «ПОСВІТ».

Irena Chawrilska / Elżbieta Czapka /
Weronika Kamińska-Skrzyńska (University of Gdańsk)

The use of microanalysis of communication in exploring conversations between migrant parents and teachers in the Pomeranian schools

Abstract

The main aim of the paper is to describe the application of microanalysis of communication in the analysis of conversations between migrant parents and teachers in Poland. Since the Russian invasion of Ukraine on Feb 24, 2022 started, Poland, due to the long border with Ukraine, cultural proximity, shared history and a large group of Ukrainian labor migrants staying in the country, became the main destination for refugees. The Polish state had to immediately include Ukrainian children in the education system. Communication between teachers and migrant children/their parents has become one of the most important challenges. Face-to-face interactions are important for development of good relationship between school and family. The cooperation between teachers and migrant parents is of fundamental significance for creating coherence in the education of the students, which is also important for the family and school (Cummins 2001).

In our research we employed a method of microanalysis of communication, which involves the close examination of actual communication sequences. Thanks to this, it is possible to analyze the empirical material (video recordings) in the microsecond scale, which allows to diagnose all elements appearing during the conversation. The analysis is multi-level and includes, among others, the verbal layer, intonation and body language. By focusing holistically on the actors involved in the conversation, the important nuances that determine the course of the conversation can be seen.

According to our knowledge, no previous research has investigated the communication process between teachers and migrant parents by using microanalysis of communication.

Historically, Poland has been a very multi-ethnic country. Due to radically altered borders, genocide, and deportations during and after the WWII, Poland became an ethnically homogenous country. However, the situation changed dramatically since the Russian invasion of Ukraine on Feb 24, 2022, when close to 16 million people had fled their homes (UNHCR, 29 November 2022). Poland, due to the long border with Ukraine, cultural proximity, shared history, and a large group of Ukrainian labor migrants staying in the country, became the main destination for war refugees.

Since 24 February 2022, 17 293 665 Ukrainians had crossed the Polish border (UNHCR, 15.12.2023). According to data from the Office for Foreigners (February 2023), almost 1 million Ukrainian citizens were under temporary protection in Poland and were given a Polish personal number (Foreign Office, February 2023). As men were not allowed to leave the country, most of the people who had left Ukraine were women with children. Approximately 87% of the Ukrainian refugees are made up of women and children, while children and teenagers account for around 43% of Ukrainian citizens holding PESEL (Foreign Office, February 2023). In the adult population, women make up approximately 77% of the total. Close to 1.4 million people have valid residence permits in the country. Ukrainians live primarily in large urban agglomerations like Warszawa, Wrocław, Kraków, Poznań, Gdańsk and Łódź.

According to data provided by the Ministry of Education and Science, there are 187.9 thousand children and youth from Ukraine in Polish schools and kindergartens who came to Poland since the war broke out (Krawczak, 2023). Based on data from the SIO database as of February 14, 2023, there are 1,792 Ukrainian teachers working in Polish schools and educational institutions (Krawczak, 2023). Among them, 1,120 teachers have been employed in schools and educational institutions since February 24, 2022. The Polish state had to immediately include Ukrainian children in the education system. The Ministry of Education and Science has undertaken several actions aimed at facilitating the admission of children and youth from Ukraine to Polish schools (Minister Edukacji i Nauki, 2022).

For a long time, Poland has been a country with a relatively low degree of cultural diversity. The teaching staff at schools were not prepared to work with pupils with minority ethnic backgrounds.

Communication between teachers, migrant children and their parents has become one of the most important challenges.

The main aim of the paper is to propose the application of microanalysis of communication in the analysis of conversations between migrant parents and teachers in Poland. According to our knowledge, no previous research has investigated the communication process between teachers and migrant parents by using microanalysis of communication in Poland.

A lot of research has been carried out on the communication between teachers and migrant parents. Face-to-face interactions are important for development of good relationship between school and family. Migrant parents are defined for the purpose of the study as parents or guardians who moved to Poland as adults with migratory experience and studying in a different school system (Antony-Newman's 2018). As research shows migrant parents have different stories behind them and educational expectations (Pananaki 2021, Vincent 2017). Studies investigating how schools meet migrant parents can contribute to ensuring equitable parental involvement. The cooperation between teachers and migrant parents is of fundamental significance for creating coherence in the education of the students, which is also important for the family and school (Cummins 2001). Dialogues, negotiations between teachers and parents promote mutual understanding and increase parents' awareness of school and local community. This might make the parents trust society more, enhance their acculturation and reduce future intergenerational conflicts (Portes & Rumbaut, 2001).

Contemporary crises and family migration

War or other catastrophic events often lead to forced migration, and in a sense all migration can be called family migration, as even individual decisions to migrate are most often made in the context of family needs and responsibilities, separating, reuniting, and reconfiguring them in many ways (Cooke 2008). In the era of polycrises: socio-economic, political, climates that generate large-scale migrations (Henig and Knight 2023), migration itself can be recognized as a crisis, as migrating individuals and families struggle with internal restrictions and conditions of entry and residence, and at the same time deal with the impact of the situation on their well-being and the resilience of the whole family. Crises can also be moments of potential change, as habitual patterns disintegrate, and social practices and institutions are reformed (Voss and Lorenz 2016). Governments resort to instruments to deal with potentially destabilizing situations. Families are forced to make quick decisions in the new reality, under new, emerging constraints, without knowing the long-term consequences of their choices (Kolbaşı-Muyan and Rittersberger-Tılıç 2023).

As in Poland we are faced with the increasing number of Ukrainians with migration experience, the situation requires new solutions for these groups of migrants. The school is one of the institutions that require special attention, as it affects the whole migrant family and the future of the youth. The demand for teaching Polish culture and language is still growing. Such a situation creates space for strategies and solutions that give us new opportunities and challenges in teaching Polish culture and language. Due to the increasing number of immigrants, Poland is becoming a multicultural and multilingual country. Polish is becoming an important language of migrants in the European Union, a bridging language between East and West (Levchuk 2020).

The complex situation of a migrant student requires a holistic approach and personalized educational, and preventive measures from educators and caregivers. Above all, the student's family situation and its dynamics must be considered when working with migrant students. However, personalization and interdisciplinarity do not exclude systemic solutions to support students and their families. A student with a migratory experience, who changes his place of residence, crosses the borders of his culture, and finally recognizes the value of being between two cultural realities trying to constitute his identity, can be shaken out of his cognitive habits and tame the new reality. Otherness still raises fears and tensions, as can easily be seen in daily acts of discrimination in the media and on the Internet. However, difficult, conflictual situations can lead to the formation of hybrid communities. The creation of concultural communities that adapt to life in Poland by participating in high culture, learning the canon of Polish culture, but not integrating with Poles, remains a threat. Learning about Polish culture does not serve migrants' co-participation in Polish culture because they are not competent to experience it, perceive it cognitively and pragmatically to understand the context and become more like Poles. Participation in popular culture is limited to one's own national circle, which creates a parallel culture to the dominant one – conculture. Migrants cultivate their own commonality without any connection to the dominant culture (Jawor, Markowska-Manista 2020).

A Systemic Model of Migrant Integration in Pomerania

An attempt to counteract the processes of conculturation in the Ukrainian community in Pomerania is a systemic model of migrant integration. Work on the Gdansk model of migrant integration began in 2015. At that time, the situation of migrants in Pomerania looked very different. Migrants made up 1% of the Pomeranian population, now it is 10%. After the outbreak of the war in Ukraine, the migrant community grew from 100,000 to at least 200,000. Migrants no longer know each other personally; but they get information from each other. Schools no longer experience the initial shock of non-Polish speaking students with a different cultural background. In such a situation, the use of mainstreaming as a tool for achieving integration proved to be crucial. Every sphere of state activity: labor market, health care, social welfare, culture, education should be inclusive (Siciarek 2022). In terms of education, this means the integration of the whole environment: from the minister to the educational staff, to the principal, to the administrative staff and, above all, to the students, teachers, and parents. Achieving this requires investment in staff competencies, materials, the development of cooperation networks, psychological diagnosis of migrant students, and effective communication with parents. In the case of Pomerania, the support is provided in a municipal-metropolitan-voivodeship model, covering more than 500 primary schools and other educational institutions, realizing the Voivodeship Development Strategy 2030 in this respect: "An important task is also the systemic integration of immigrants. Economic, cultural-social, legal-institutional, identity and spatial integration measures must be taken, which should lead to immigrants having rights, opportunities, and services available to all residents of the province" (SRWP 2021).

For migrant parents in particular, the inclusive approach is about bringing them into the existing life of the school, giving them access to it, and making them feel a part of it. Often this means changing the way things are done, so schools are sometimes reluctant to make this kind of change, relying instead on one-off workshops or inclusion meetings for parents. However, migrant parents should be included in all the opportunities that are not available to them due to lack of information or other barriers.[1] It should not be the case that migrants look for Ukrainian-friendly schools in Facebook groups. They should know that every school in the region follows the same standards and in every school their child will go through the same process and they themselves will be involved in the process under the same conditions. An example of this type of activity is the welcome package prepared for Pomeranian migrant students and migrant parents in different language versions, which aims to remove the basic barriers caused by differences in educational systems and school customs.[2]

Another model example of support for institutional change is the Pomorskie Centrum Edukacji Nauczycieli w Gdańsku (Pomeranian Centre for Teacher Education in Gdańsk), which in 2021 launched a multi-year program to increase the capacity of schools to educate and integrate students with migration experience. The pilot involved 30 schools, each with 7–8 trainees (37 hours of training for principals, tutors, subject and Polish language teachers). Intercultural communication training not only with students but also with migrant parents should be an important part of this kind of training. The analysis of the training programs shows that this issue is present in the courses. The trainers rely on the procedures for admitting immigrant students to the school and on their own experience in communicating with immigrant parents, without referring to research in this field, as none has been done.

The activities carried out by PCEN are part of a systemic model for the integration of migrants, which is still lacking, especially regarding educational issues. Concerts and multicultural picnics are easily promoted as integration policies, but more crucial is systemic integration that serves all migrants, not just those who participate in projects. It is important that through systemic measures migrant parents understand that systemic solutions have been prepared for them and that schools have an integration and not an assimilation bias.

On forming learning communities

Creating learning communities also requires the involvement and presence of migrant parents. They are an important link in the process of learning and exploring the world for every young person. The learning process is not only between student and teacher, but migrant parents are also part of this process. Exploring the idea of re-scaping (Van der Tuin, Verhoeff 2021), learning communities embracing migrants and non-migrants should aim to deal with the mental, social, and environmental challenges of the present by interventions designed locally.

First, it should be noted that regardless of the events that make up the instability of the outside world, the broadest group of identified risk factors for poor mental health among youth are related to school performance, school stress, falling behind in school and the difficulties in overcoming them. Interestingly, the outbreak of war in Ukraine did not add to the mental problems of youth, in the first year of the war, the intake action in schools was not associated with side effects that would place an undue burden on the hosts. As the research shows, the most important source of mental health protection for students in a changing reality (epidemics, changes in the teaching mode, war in Ukraine, etc.) is the size, quality, and availability of the support network. The closest and most basic elements of the social support network are related to parents and family, peers and teachers and educators (Jak wspierać młodzież w niestabilnym świecie 2023).

Strengthening the psychological well-being of young people can be much more effective if the needs of parents and teachers are considered, and if good relationships are maintained throughout the young person's environment. The school environment is an interconnected system. Strengthening one element strengthens the others. In the current realities of an unstable world, practical actions that intentionally strengthen all groups in the school environment (students, parents, teachers) and improve their relationships with each other are particularly valuable. Building mental resilience in children and adolescents, as one of the most important competencies for functioning in a complex and unstable world, is now a fundamental challenge for educational and preventive work. Strengthening the psyche, hardening the body and the mind requires understanding and acceptance of this need on the part of parents and support from educators, school specialists and preventionists.

On designing learning activities embracing students, teachers, parents

Nowadays in Poland learning activities, including foreign language classes aimed at improving intercultural competence due to the number of migrants, that integrate cultural and linguistic aspects to better understand the place we live, the community that we are part of not to experience social detachment particularly when we are the part of a hybrid community. Focusing on questions bothering us in today's everyday life, immersing ourselves in a glocal perspective, considering together if learning activities respond to global challenges, and how they address the issues of building resilience and well-being seems to be super important within school groups in which very often nowadays 15 students come from Poland and 15 are migrants. Young people in the Tri-city area experience all the problems afflicting young people today, which makes them a vulnerable and sensitive group. Through well-designed learning activities embracing students, teachers, and parents it is possible to aim to think ecologically as Guattari states (Guattari 2008), building resilience and well-being with reference to more-than-human thinking and Gdansk heritage. Designing appropriate learning activities to enable the creation of hybrid learning communities that are also support networks, considering parents in an era of uncertainty resulting from the crises of the modern world, should be the goal of educational organizations working with students and parents experiencing migration.

To create good learning communities, we need to map barriers and facilitators in communication between migrant parents and teachers. Microanalysis of communication can be useful in identifying gaps in the conversation process and designing such communication and educational solutions that will facilitate the learning process and the process of integration and adaptation to Polish conditions.

Microanalysis method

Micro-level conversation analysis began to develop in the 1980s (Bavelas et al. 1987; Kendon, 1997; HZ Li, 1999). Scientists (e. g., psychologists, psychiatrists) noticed that certain communication elements (such as gestures, facial expressions, or words used) may affect the effectiveness of conversations, including those of a professional nature, such as psychotherapy sessions (Bavelas et al. 2000). Currently, the method is increasingly recognized by other scientific branches as a helpful tool of both cognitive and practical nature. Conversational microanalysis is popular in health sciences, where it examines doctor-patient relationships or specific groups of patients (for example, people with autism) (Bavelas et al. 2017; Gerwing, 2008). In the context of the doctor-patient relationship, the method examines, for example, in what situations misunderstandings occur in a conversation with a migrant patient, or how the gestures used by both parties are read (are they perceived in the same way by both parties or are they due to differences culturally, a given gesture has a different meaning, whether the gesture helps or rather disrupts the conversation) (Gerwing, Dalby, 2014). An interesting use of this method is also the study by Svane and colleagues (2021), in which the authors checked how during direct conversations parent and child influence each other's autobiographical memory, including its changes, or deepening the memorization of repeated and consistent information.

What is the method and what is the analysis process?

The method involves a detailed analysis of the course of a conversation between at least two individuals. The conversation is recorded in video format and then exported to the ELAN program, which is freely available online (Bavelas et al., 2017). This type of analysis requires high precision, focus and a lot of time. As part of the analysis of the video recording, researchers can create a "layer" dedicated to the topic that the researchers are particularly interested in – for example, linking specific words spoken with the gesture used by the interlocutor. The same applies to body language and facial expressions. Thanks to the ELAN program, you can see in milliseconds how a given unit's operation is changing. The researchers can also select only those fragments that are the most interesting for them and focus on them by playing them in repetition, or they can easily search for an interesting fragment by keywords used in the layers in ELAN.

Considering that the image of individuals is visible in the recording, and the topics discussed may sometimes concern personal data or sensitive content, it is important to obtain consent from the ethics committee at a university, as well as from the institutions that will participate in the study (e. g., a high school). A big challenge is also to obtain consent from the people the researchers want to analyze – the participants in the conversation. In this type of project, the researchers do not directly participate in the conversation, they are not even its observers. The task of the research team is only technical supervision before and after the video recording (i. e., appropriate setting of the camera, chairs, or light), because it is important that the conversation has the character of a real conversation. Also, the topics discussed during the conversation cannot be directed or constructed by the researcher – in this case participants will discuss school life, subjects, or other school-related activities. Thanks to this, researchers can discover at what moments in the conversation the parent migrant feels comfortable talking to the teacher, and which elements cause difficulties or misunderstandings for one of the parties. As indicated at the beginning, the technique may prove to be extremely important for people who have been in Poland for a short time and for whom Polish or English is not their native language. Sometimes a certain verbal context used may be different from the reference from the home country known to migrants, which may result in misapprehension or even cause conflict (Nissen, Meuter, 2023). Similarly, the use of certain words, including epistemic adverbs, may have no equivalents in the migrant's country of origin (Nissen, Meuter, 2023).

Conclusions

Access to education is one of the dimensions of structural integration of migrants. In most countries migrant children are entitled to education, however, access remains difficult. Migrants may face cultural, economic, or practical barriers to effectively exercise their right to education. Lack of knowledge or insufficient knowledge of the language of the country of immigration is one of the most common barriers in access to education. This applies not only to migrant pupils themselves, but also to their parents, who are an important element in successful education of migrant children. Therefore, it is necessary to look at communication between migrant parents and teachers, identify challenges and develop methods to deal with these challenges.

The article proposes a method of micro-analysis of communication in order to study communication challenges in conversations between migrant parents and schoolteachers in Poland. This method of analyzing communication has not been used in such a context before, hence the proposed research is pioneering. A detailed research methodology and results will be presented in another article.

Bibliography

Antony-Newman, M. (2018). Parental involvement of immigrant parents: A meta-synthesis. *Educ. Rev.* 71, 362–381. doi: 10.1080/00131911.2017.1423278.

Bavelas, J. B. (2000). Microanalysis of Communication in Psychotherapy. Janet Beavin Bavelas, Dan McGee, Bruce Phillips, and Robin Routledge.

Bavelas, J. B., Black, A., Lemery, C. R., Mullett, J., Eisenberg, N., & Strayer, J. (1987). Empathy and its development. *Motor mimicry as primitive empathy*, 317–338.

Bavelas, J., Gerwing, J., Healing, S., & Tomori, C. (2017). Microanalysis of Face-to-Face Dialogue (MFD). *The sourcebook of listening research: Methodology and measures*, 445–452.

Cooke, T. J. (2008). Migration in a family way. *Population, Space and Place*, 14(4), 255–265. doi:10.1002/psp.500.

Cummins, J. (2001). Empowering minority students: A framework for intervention. *Harvard Educational Review*, *71*(4), 649–675.

Gerwing, J. (2008). *Quantifying infant social responsiveness: Microanalysis of home videos of a set of triplets for early indications of autism* (Doctoral dissertation).

Gerwing, J., & Dalby, A. M. L. (2014). Gestures convey content: An exploration of the semantic functions of physicians' gestures. *Patient education and counseling*, *96*(3), 308–314.

Guattari, F. (2008) The Three Ecologies. Continuum, London.

Henig D., Knight D. M. (2023) 'Polycrisis: Prompts for an Emerging Worldview', *Anthropology Today*, 39/2: 3–6.

http://Pismo_Pana_Ministra_Przemys%C5%82awa_Czarnka_do_dyr_szk%C3%B3%C5 %82,_kurator%C3%B3w_i_samorz%C4%85dowc%C3%B3w-1.pdf (accessed: 30.10. 2023).

https://data.unhcr.org/en/situations/ukraine (accessed: 19.02.2024).

https://fdds.pl/_Resources/Persistent/5/e/8/9/5e8940d252b5fdcadd95e8a2d5a2daea07b11 e29/Dzieci%20si%C4%99%20licz%C4%85%202022%20-%20Ukraina.pdf (accessed: 30.10.2023).

https://www.gov.pl/web/udsc/obywatele-ukrainy-w-polsce-aktualne-dane-migracyjne2 (accessed: 24.02.2023).

Jak wspierać mlodzież w niestabilnym świecie 2023, https://ipzin.org/wp-content/upload s/2023/05/Raport-2023-Jak-wspierac-mlodziez-ONLINE_1.pdf (accessed: 19.02.2024).

Jawor A., Markowska-Manista U. (2020). Konkultura. Wymiary uczestnictwa w kulturze młodych imigrantów z Ukrainy w Polsce, Warszawa: Wydawnictwo Naukowe Scholar.

Kendon, A. (1997). Gesture. *Annual review of anthropology*, *26*(1), 109–128.

Kolbaşı-Muyan G., Rittersberger-Tılıç H. (2023). 'Birth of a Virtual Community: Supporting Turkish Couples' Migration during COVID-19', *Family Relations*, 72/2: 478–94.

Krawczak, A. (2022). Sytuacja dzieci ukraińskich w Polsce. Dzieci się liczą 2022. Raport o zagrożeniach bezpieczeństwa i rozwoju dzieci w Polsce, Fundacja Dajemy Dzieciom Siłę.

Levchuk, P. (2020) *Trójjęzyczność ukraińsko-rosyjsko-polska w Ukraińców niepolskiego pochodzenia,* Kraków: Księgarnia Akdemicka.

Li, H. Z. (1999). Grounding and information communication in intercultural and intracultural dyadic discourse. *Discourse Processes*, *28*(3), 195–215.

Nissen, V., & Meuter, R. F. (2023). The impact of bilinguality and language context on the understanding of epistemic adverbs in health communication: the case of English and Russian. *Frontiers in Psychology*, *14*, 1179341.

OECD (2018), Working Together for Local Integration of Migrants and Refugees, OECD Publishing, Paris. http://dx.doi.org/10.1787/9789264085350-en.

Pananaki, M. (2021). *The Parent–Teacher Encounter: A (mis)match between habitus and doxa*(Doctoral dissertation). Stockholm: Stockholm University. Available online at: http:// www.diva-portal.org/smash/get/diva2:1544222/FULLTEXT01.pdf (accessed: 19.02.2024).

Portes, A., & Rumbaut, R. G. (2001). *Legacies: the story of the immigrant second generation.* Berkeley: Russell Sage Foundation.

Siciarek M. (2022). Pomorskie doświadczenia integracji migrantów, https://www.kongre sobywatelski.pl/wp-content/uploads/2022/08/ko-ptl-2-2022-marta_siciarek-pomorski e_doswiadczenia_integracji_migrantow.pdf (accessed: 19.02.2024).

Strategia Rozwoju Województwa Pomorskiego https://porp.pl/uploads/original/042021/1 3/22732a9117_Zalacznik-do-uchwaly_SWP_376_XXXI_21_SRWP2030_120421.pdf (accessed: 19.02.2024).

Svane, R. P., Kingo, O. S., & Krøjgaard, P. (2021). A micro-analytic approach to parent-child reminiscing. *Cognitive Development*, *57*, 101004.

Van der Tuin, I. and N. Verhoeff. (2021). Critical Concepts for the Creative Humanities. Rowman and Littlefield International, London.

Vincent, C. (2017). 'The children have only got one education and you have to make sure it's a good one': Parenting and parent–school relations in a neoliberal age. *Gender Educ.* 29, 541–557. doi: 10.1080/09540253.2016.1274387.

Voss M., Lorenz D. S. (2016) 'Sociological Foundations of Crisis Communication'. In: Schwarz A., Seegar M. W., Auer C. (eds) *The Handbook of International Crisis Communication Research*, pp. 45–54. Chichester: Wiley Blackwell.

Zbigniew Szmyt (Adam Mickiewicz University in Poznań)

Schools for Immigrants: Educational Migration and Learning Polish at Private Colleges. A Case Study of the City of Poznań[1]

Abstract

The paper explores the institutionalized transmission of migrant knowledge within vocational colleges, focusing on a case study in Poznań, Poland, primarily serving immigrants from Ukraine and Belarus. Through ethnographic fieldwork conducted between 2022 and 2023, including participant observation and interviews, the research illuminates the process of teaching the Polish language in a migrant environment without the involvement of native speakers. Findings reveal a focus on practical language skills and the sharing of experiential knowledge, fostering socio-linguistic integration. The study underscores the significance of vocational colleges in the integration process and highlights the potential for inter-migrant transmission of language skills within these institutions. This study contributes to a deeper understanding of the dynamics of educational migration and language acquisition among immigrants in Poland.

Introduction

For some reason, vocational colleges, being post-secondary schools, usually fall outside the focus of migration researchers and glottodidactics, even though this type of school is the prevalent form of language and vocational education among refugees and immigrants from Ukraine. Meanwhile, researchers focus on primary and secondary schools and higher education institutions. The peripheral status of vocational colleges is visible in statistics, where scholars typically do not distinguish this category, making it unclear whether colleges are classified as a form of higher education or as secondary education.

The paper explores a seldom-examined topic: the instruction of the Polish language to Ukrainians in private vocational schools. This education mode, accessible to individuals over 18, stands out as an affordable and highly accessible

1 This article is the result of research conducted as part of the project titled "Mapping of new agents and tendencies in tuition of Polish as a foreign language among Ukrainian immigrants in Poland", implemented under the NAWA Intervention Grant BPN/GIN/2022/1/00088.

avenue for vocational and language education for foreigners. The specificity of the vocational schools under study is their focus on catering to students from former Soviet countries. The research aims to illuminate: 1) the significance of vocational colleges in the educational migration process; 2) the methodologies and effectiveness of teaching and learning the Polish language within these institutions; 3) the sociolinguistic implications of widespread education of Ukrainians in vocational colleges.

Research Methodology

The essential qualitative data were collected through ethnographic field research conducted in Poznań between 2022 and 2023. The research methodologies included interviews with lecturers and students from vocational schools. From September 1, 2022, to November 30, 2022, the researcher engaged in participant observation in a massage therapy class, attending both theoretical and practical sessions three times a week. In February 2023, a second series of observations took place in the same group. Additionally, the researcher adopted the "mystery shopper" method by enrolling as a regular student and disclosing to interested peers that their research focused on migrations at the Center for Migration Studies at Adam Mickiewicz University. This long-term immersion in the group as a student facilitated the observation of the actual teaching and learning process of the Polish language. Interactions with participants both within and outside the school facilitated the conduction of unstructured interviews and active engagement in the Polish language acquisition process.

Structure of the Studied Group

The case study revolves around one of the largest vocational colleges for foreigners in Poznań, where over 90% of students hail from post-Soviet countries, primarily Ukraine and Belarus. Nearly all teaching, administrative, and cleaning staff are migrants from the former USSR. The school was founded by a female immigrant from Kazakhstan of Polish descent, who, upon arriving in Poland, graduated from a massage school. She then purchased a struggling non-profit vocational college and restructured it into a centre for paramedical professions catering to Russian and Ukrainian-speaking students. Over time, the school expanded its curriculum to encompass other professions, and recently, it inaugurated a vocational-technical school primarily attended by teenagers from Ukraine. The school has a branch in Bydgoszcz – another provincial capital. While Polish students do enrol, their numbers are limited, and they often face integration challenges within the predominantly Russian-speaking student body, frequently turning to teachers for assistance due to their lack of proficiency in Russian.

Initially, my class consisted of over 50 individuals, but within two months, it halved in size. Aside from myself, there were two Polish students and one from Kazakhstan, while the rest hailed from Ukraine and Belarus. Given that the college catered to adults, the age range within the group varied from 18 to 50 years old, with differing lengths of residency in Poland and varying language proficiencies. Over half of the group had recently arrived in Poland and confessed to not knowing the Polish language during the initial classes. The remaining students possessed limited Polish language skills, acquired either through work or short-term language courses in Poznań. While most lacked higher education, some had obtained degrees in their home countries. Most were engaged in manual labour in production or the service sector. For many, their only exposure to learning a foreign language was through studying English in school, though proficiency was generally low, necessitating basic English classes. Although Ukrainian students predominantly spoke Russian, they exhibited varying degrees of proficiency in Ukrainian.

Migration Processes and Private Schooling

The shape of contemporary immigration to Poland has been significantly influenced by the political transformation initiated in 1989, Poland's accession to the European Union in 2004, and the war in Ukraine. Following the collapse of communism, Poland witnessed increasing immigration flows, initially characterised by the return of Polish expatriates and the influx of individuals seeking economic opportunities. In the early years, immigration was predominantly labour-oriented, driven by demand for construction, agriculture, and service workers. However, immigration patterns diversified over time, encompassing family reunification, asylum-seeking (mostly Armenians from Nagorno Karabakh and Chechens from Russia), and international student migration (Czerniejewska 2016: 619). Regional and global dynamics have influenced immigration to Poland. Due to their historical ties and geographical proximity, neighbouring countries such as Ukraine, Belarus, and Russia constituted primary sources of immigrants. Poland witnessed changing migration patterns, including increased immigration from Eastern Europe and other EU countries after it acceded to the European Union in 2004.

Before 2022, the largest group of foreigners in Poland were economic migrants, and refugees formed a relatively small group – mostly because of Poland's anti-refugee policy, reluctance to accept refugees, particularly from Muslim-majority countries, and a focus on border security. Economic migrants arrived in Poland for short- or long-term stays for employment purposes, and they stayed in the country based on a work visa, temporary or permanent residence permit, or a long-term EU resident permit. As of early 2022, Poland was home to over 2 million immigrants, with around 1.5 million from Ukraine. Other significant nationalities included Belarusians, Germans, Moldovans, Russians, and Indians. This figure contrasts with a decade ago when Poland had approximately 100,000 immigrants, mainly from former Soviet countries. It indicates a significant shift in Poland's migration status over the past decade, transforming it from having one of the lowest immigrant shares in the EU to becoming a European leader, especially in terms of migrant worker influx. As a result of Russia's full-scale aggression against Ukraine, millions of refugees have arrived in Poland. At its peak in May 2022, Poland was home to 3.4 million refugees (Jarosz, Klaus 2022:23). By early 2024, this number had dropped to 955,110 people[2]. With 190,000 Ukrainian students enrolled in Polish schools by February 2023, Poland's education system faced challenges due to language barriers and the ongoing conflict in Ukraine. It is estimated that about half of the school-aged refugees from Ukraine study remotely in Ukrainian schools and do not attend Polish educational institutions (Bloch, Szmyt 2024: 29).

Parallel to public schools and universities in Poland, the private school sector is developing, which, due to its pro-market orientation, often demonstrates greater flexibility and quickly reorients itself to the needs of refugees and immigrants. Non-public education operates at all levels of education: primary schools, secondary schools, vocational colleges (post-secondary schools), and higher education institutions. Since the 1990s, the private education market has been developing dynamically, and in 2011, almost 50% of higher education students were enrolled in non-public institutions. During this time, 6,200 foreigners studied in the non-public sector – 34% of all international students (Geryk 2011: 140).

The private sector attempted to compete with public institutions and occupied new educational niches. Primary and secondary schools specialised in more elitist education or progressive pedagogical programs, mainly targeting the needs of the affluent middle class. With the influx of expatriates in larger cities, English-language schools for foreign children emerged, where Polish was taught as a foreign language. At the regional level, an example of such a school is the International School of Poznań, where over 600 people from Poland and abroad are educated.

The years 1990–2006 were a period of private higher education boom. In the academic year 1992/93, there were 18 private universities in Poland educating just

---

2 https://www.consilium.europa.eu/pl/infographics/ukraine-refugees-eu/.

over 16,000 students. However, ten years later, there were already 252 non-public higher education institutions, with nearly 530,000 students enrolled. Due to demographic decline, the number of students decreased significantly in later years, resulting in the closure of smaller private educational institutions (Stachowicz 2013: 63–65). Nowadays, out of 349 higher education institutions in Poland, 219 are private (Cudzoziemcy…2023).

As the number of Polish students declined, the expanded academic structures began to vie for international students by implementing international exchange programs and recruiting foreigners for paid programs conducted in English or Polish. Studies in Poland became quite attractive after Poland acceded to the EU due to relatively low costs and the possibility of legalising one's stay and accessing the job market, as student status allows for employment (Boichuk 2023: 147–150). Between 2000/2001 and 2021/2022, the number of foreigners enrolled in studies in Poland surged from 6,563 to 105,400. Students from Ukraine in 2022 accounted for 48,149 individuals, which is 46 per cent of all foreign students. Together with 180,000 Ukrainian students in lower levels of education, this gives a total of approximately 228,000 Ukrainian citizens studying in the Polish education system. Some private colleges rely almost exclusively on students from abroad – mainly from outside the EU. The existence of higher education institutions for foreigners has recently become a subject of media discussion:

> According to figures from the Ministry of Education and Science for the year 2020 at the Higher School of Internal Security in Łódź, out of 2,499 registered students, 2,492 are foreigners, with only seven being Polish. The Polonia Academy in Częstochowa educates 1,023 students, of which 859 are foreigners. Similarly, at the Vistula University School of Tourism and Hospitality in Warsaw, out of 1,229 students, a staggering 825 are foreigners. At the Academy of Hotel Management and Catering Industry in Poznań, out of 579 students, 371 come from abroad. Colleges boasting international students exceeding 50 per cent are the Warsaw School of Business, Wrocław University of Economics, and the Wincenty Pol University of Social and Natural Sciences in Lublin (Mirowska-Łoskot 2021; cf. Cudzoziemcy… 2023).

Foreigners in the school system were perceived as an integration problem, while in higher education, they were seen as an indicator of prestige and the internationalisation of universities. Institutions dedicated to students from less affluent countries of Eastern Europe, Turkey, and Africa are viewed with suspicion, either as schemes serving migration flows or as diploma mills.

Educational Migration to Poznań

In Poznań, the sector of accessible, low-budget education for foreigners quickly came to dominate private universities and schools. Primary and secondary schools specialised in more elitist education or progressive pedagogical programs, mainly targeting the needs of the affluent middle class. With the influx of expatriates in larger cities, English-language schools for foreign children emerged, where Polish was taught as a foreign language. At the regional level, an example of such a school is the International School of Poznań, which currently educates over 600 children from Poland and abroad. However, the largest expansion of private education services occurred in post-secondary and higher education school sectors, for which students from outside the EU became the main and sometimes the sole target group. Educational migrations have become a popular migration strategy, whereby private universities offer vocational training, Polish language learning, residence legalisation, health insurance, student status granting access to the job market, and often even a network of contacts with employers. Several schools effectively serve as commercial labour intermediaries between non-EU labour and employers in the EU. In Poznań, such a school is the Academy of Hotel Management and Catering Industry, where students primarily from the CIS countries and Ukraine studied and who, as part of their professional internships during the tourist season, worked in hotels in France, Luxembourg, Spain, Italy, Ireland, Norway, Austria, Greece, and even Cyprus, Turkey, or the United Arab Emirates.

A crucial legal regulation affecting the popularity of often low-quality schools is the requirement to obtain, along with the diploma confirming the graduation from school, certification of proficiency in the Polish language at the B1 level necessary for applying for temporary residence permits, permanent residence, or citizenship. My interlocutors – international students of vocational post-secondary schools – emphasised that obtaining a B1 certificate without needing a difficult state exam weighed heavily on their decision to pursue education at a vocational school. It is also an important pull factor for older students who have often completed a full educational cycle in their home country and have been professionally active there for years. Another attractive factor respondents mentioned is the low tuition fees, which are partially subsidised by the state budget:

> I'm 37 years old, I work in a warehouse, and I'm interested in massage. I'd like to learn this profession because I can't physically work in a warehouse forever. This school is perfect for me – classes are in the evenings or on weekends, they'll teach me Polish, and you don't have to take the B1 exam for this school. Half of the people signed up here just to avoid taking that exam. It's a shame they introduced tuition fees – 150 PLN [35 euro]

per month this year. It used to be free – I signed up last year but didn't attend because I had too much work[3].

Private vocational colleges (post-secondary schools in Polish terminology) have become institutions supporting the legalisation, socio-economical adaptation, and learning of the Polish language. However, this adaptation and learning of Polish occur in conditions different from public schools and universities. We are dealing with a segmented adaptation model, where new immigrants are incorporated into an older immigrant segment within the society rather than into the mainstream Polish culture. (cf. Wimmer 2007:4). This phenomenon should be considered procedurally as an adaptive strategy in the initial stage of socio-economic integration. Below, an analysis of methods and specifics of teaching the Polish language in private vocational schools oriented towards students from Ukraine and Belarus will be presented.

Case Study – Learning Polish in Massage Classes

The massage therapy program was structured into practical and theoretical classes. The theoretical courses covered anatomy, massage techniques, entrepreneurship basics, first aid, and English language. Practical sessions focused on practising massage techniques under the supervision of Ms. Ludmila, a lecturer from Russia with many years of residency in Poland. Students could participate in Polish language lessons twice a week as part of the curriculum. These sessions were conducted remotely by lecturers who were not native speakers. Students who attended these classes complained about the large group sizes and were not highly impressed by the quality of the lessons. Nevertheless, they tried to participate actively, as learning the language was a priority for many. None of the lecturers were Polish; the faculty hailed from Ukraine, Belarus, and, to a lesser extent, Russia. The presence of lecturers who were also immigrants was significantly meaningful for the students, fostering a sense of cultural intimacy (Herzfeld 1997) through shared language, cultural space participation, and migratory experiences. These lecturers, seen as confident and successful in their social and economic integration, became role models for students, who often sought advice based on their experiences adapting to Polish society. Inquiries about how the lecturers learned Polish and how quickly they did so were frequent.

Officially, the school's sole instructional language was Polish. However, this policy was not strictly enforceable when most of the group did not understand

---

3 Interview conducted in Ukrainian, Poznań, 14.09.2022, male, 37 years old, Ukrainian.

Polish, as was the case with my group. During our first class, Ms Ludmila informed us in Russian not to worry if we did not speak the language yet, sharing her own experience of arriving without Polish language skills, training as a masseuse, and learning Polish within a few months. She indicated that initial classes would be partly in Russian and would gradually transit into Polish.

During the theoretical classes, lecturers used presentations in Polish, but in the first month, they often conducted most of the classes in Russian. It caused frustration among the two Polish students, who did not always understand what was being discussed. Typically, lecturers would explain in Russian what material would be covered and then discuss the topic in Polish, using the presentation's text for support. However, students who did not understand Polish quickly began asking questions in Ukrainian and Russian. The lecturers usually responded in Russian and often forgot to switch back to Polish. In the first month of classes, a dynamic trilingualism operated, with Ukrainian, Polish, and Russian languages being used interchangeably (cf. Levchuk 2020). At the same time, Polish specialised terms in speech and writing were consistently anchored in the respective classes – economic terms in entrepreneurship basics, medical terms in first aid classes, and anatomical terms and disease units in massage classes. Great importance was attached to the use of Polish professional terminology. The lecturers emphasised this because these terms were required for the state vocational exam at the end of the studies. Gradually, as students began to understand Polish better, a larger portion of the classes were conducted in Polish. As a native Polish speaker, I initially found the lecturers' Russian accent and their phonetic and grammatical mistakes amusing, but the lecturers seemed unconcerned by this. Our group's supervisor explained that:

> You are not a philologist, and you do not have to speak Polish perfectly – no one expects that from you. You need to learn how to communicate effectively and master the Polish professional terminology so that you can serve clients effectively and pass the state exam. Don't worry about mistakes or the accent – I will understand you anyway. You need to speak as much as possible, and you will see that by the second semester, you will be speaking Polish.

The students responded very enthusiastically to these kinds of instructions. In a conversation after class, several of them told me that the fact our lecturers are not Poles but learned Polish themselves, just as they are now, makes them feel unafraid to attempt speaking Polish. The lecturers placed significant emphasis on verifying the assimilation of theoretical material. It had to be presented publicly in Polish. Regular tests were also conducted in Polish, during which internet resources or notes were tacitly tolerated. This approach made the tests resemble more of a review session and exercise in writing in Polish.

The transitional phase of the group's transition to Polish was a pidgin, within which the syntax and lexicon of the three languages were mixed. A working pidgin (as opposed to descriptive grammar, which nobody knew or used) became the de facto metalanguage in which the proper Polish language was discussed. The emergence of such a this pidgin was facilitated by the allowance for communication in native languages with the strict requirement to use Polish industry-specific terms. The pidgin phase did not surprise the lecturers. After establishing Polish terminology, they began to correct the most incomprehensible grammatical forms and language clichés from the perspective of the Polish language.

Initially, I critically approached the assumptions of this type of language acquisition. However, during my follow-up visit to the group in the second semester of teaching, the classes were mostly conducted in Polish, and the students could communicate in Polish and take notes from the classes in this language.

For the assimilation of the Polish language, practical sessions were also important, during which students regularly conducted simulations of serving a Polish-speaking client – from reception, through medical interviews, stages of massage, to the financial settlement of the service. Students also had to describe the procedures they performed in Polish during the massage, including medical contraindications for various forms of massage, etc. Thus, two types of simulations took place: working in a massage parlour and the state vocational exam. Both simulations were dynamic, with role-playing and significant student engagement. In the customer service simulation, students had the greatest freedom in choosing phrases and conducting casual conversations with the massaged client. The practical classes were met with the greatest enthusiasm, and it was during these sessions that students asked the most questions about how to say something in Polish and what norms of social interaction prevailed in Poland.

My observations and the lecturers' statements were confirmed in a programmatic interview given by the college's founder:

> How can one learn Polish by attending Polish language classes? It's simple math – 19 hours a week of classes in floristry in Polish. In these classes, you listen, speak, and write in Polish for 19 hours a week for four weeks, plus 2 hours of Polish language classes twice a week – covering grammar, syntax, spelling, and punctuation. That adds up to 19 hours + 4 hours. Multiply this by the number of weeks in a semester, and even if a student meets the minimum attendance requirement – 51%, it results in a significant amount of Polish language instruction – over 300 hours per semester. In any case, a person will achieve the B1 level. Our students pass the state exam in Polish, write by hand in this language, and answer questions[4].

---

4 Graduate's interview with the college owner (in Russian): *Pereekhala v Pol'shu i osnovala politseal'nuyu shkolu Medicus. Interv'yu s Tat'yana Yerofeyevoy*, https://www.youtube.com/wa tch?v=1NDtc95-8ng (accessed: 14.02.224).

In the interview, Ms. Tatiana shares her experience of studying massage therapy in Poland, learning the language, and how she decided with a friend to use their migratory adaptation experiences to create a school that meets immigrants' linguistic and integration needs. According to her, besides preparing for a profession, European education teaches immigrants the Polish language and legal and social realities in the host country, enabling graduates to navigate Polish society effectively. hus, we are dealing with the intentional use of accumulated migrant knowledge (cf. Williams 2007) in a business model aimed at vocational education for foreigners. Ms. Tatiana is aware that a significant percentage of students enrol in the school to legalise their stay, obtain work permits, learn the Polish language, and acquire a language certificate. She views her college as an institution fulfilling an integrative mission for immigrants from the East. In the last year, the school's management has launched a PR campaign among officials dealing with migration issues, presenting their know-how in the field of education and integration of refugees and immigrants.

Confrontational case – Vocational High School for Adults in Poznań

The teaching paradigm and acquisition of the Polish language described above, utilising the knowledge of migrant teaching staff, is not employed in all vocational schools. In a vocational high school for adults located in Poznań, no language or adaptation programs for foreigners were introduced for quite some time:

> Our high school was established with working Poles in mind, who could obtain a diploma and professional qualifications needed for further career development by attending classes every other weekend. Before 2022, each class had 2–3 Ukrainians or Belarusians, but no one really paid any attention to it. They had to learn Polish independently, or they wouldn't pass the final exams. Since the start of the war, there has been a massive enrollment of Ukrainians because, along with the diploma, they obtain a certificate of Polish language proficiency at the B1 level – they need this for the Polish Card and residence permit. Instead of attending expensive courses, they can gain professional qualifications (massage therapist, ward assistant, safety inspector, IT technician) at the B1 level. Initially, we didn't organise any Polish language courses, and after many months, the administration organised some additional lessons, probably paid and outside the regular class schedule. And this is a real problem. In some groups, we have up to 80% foreigners aged 30–50. Most of them hardly know any Polish, yet the classes are in this language. It's clear that the teaching level is low, but somehow, they have to pass the vocational exam at the end of their studies. Many people struggle with the alphabet, unable to switch from Cyrillic to the Latin alphabet. They learn to speak over time, but probably because they work with Poles, as you can't learn much from attending classes two days a month. Overall, our administration noticed that as the

number of interested Poles decreases, the number of students from Ukraine and Belarus increases, and they are becoming our target group. The school's website was translated into Ukrainian, but no one is particularly concerned with teaching them Polish. People sit in class, and when the lecturer asks them a question, it usually ends with a few minutes of confusion on both sides – because the student and lecturer don't understand each other – they speak different languages. It's quite awkward that lecturers usually avoid these situations – it's too stressful for both parties. I probably don't need to add that the teachers were unprepared to work with foreigners and are not additionally compensated for it. They usually just don't engage with individuals who speak Polish poorly[5].

Also, in this case, students from Ukraine and other post-Soviet countries have become the main client base of the private vocational school for adults. However, the school has not made significant efforts to adapt the curriculum and educational techniques for Ukrainian and Russian-speaking individuals. Teachers do not know the students' native languages and are not trained to work with such students, nor do they consider teaching the Polish language as one of the classes' objectives. The schedule of sessions, which take place every two weeks, also hinders regular contact with the language and reinforcement of the learned content.

Conclusion – Institutionalised Migrant Knowledge

The case of a vocational college founded and run by integrated immigrants for new immigrants can be seen as an example of the institutionalised inter-generational transmission of migrant knowledge. The business model, based on immigrants from Ukraine and Belarus as the main target group, assumes openness to the integrative needs of immigrants – language learning, obtaining a language certificate, legalising stay, and professional activation. Thanks to cultural intimacy, teachers become adaptive role models for students, actively providing them with biographical examples from their own experiences concerning mistakes, language misunderstandings, and methods of acquiring the Polish language.

In the realm of language learning, migrant knowledge forms a comprehensive conceptual category that includes both the biographies of learners and the beliefs and subjective theories they have developed. Its scope is significantly wider, ranging from basic information about travelling to the host country, navigating legalisation procedures, understanding labour market regulations, assessing costs, identifying public utilities, obtaining discounts, navigating social pro-

---

5 Interview with Adam – Lecturer, Poznań, 4.12.2023.

grams and engaging with cultural and entertainment activities. This knowledge is a collective and interconnected resource of experiences, insights, and information co-created and shared among migrants to enhance their functionality in a foreign country. Migrant knowledge is propagated through direct interactions, particularly in acquiring Polish as a foreign language, which encompasses practical advice and sharing experiences.

A new sociolinguistic phenomenon is occurring, in which older migrants teach Polish to the newly arrived – linguistically and socially socialising them based on their own experiences. The Polish language begins to function and be taught without the involvement of native speakers and professional lecturers. Language learning is adapted to immigrants' needs and adaptive strategies, most of whom represent the working class. Most of my respondents declared a need for communicative knowledge of Polish, and teachers did not instil in them a pursuit of linguistic purism. The primary criterion was communicative success with precise use of professional terminology. Under such conditions, the range of acceptable phonetic realisations of Polish words, grammar, and lexicon naturally changes. In a trilingual environment, language interference inevitably occurs, which has the character of a temporary pidgin. Still, some interferences may become rooted at the group level in Polish/Ukrainian/Russian.

The vocational college serves adults of working age who have limited opportunities for learning the Polish language and profession due to their economic situation. It is an institution that integrates immigrants at the initial stage of this process. The case studies presented in this paper do not provide a comprehensive picture of the process of teaching Polish in post-secondary schools. Still, they clearly show the potential and trends forming in the institutionalised intermigrant transmission of language skills.

Bibliography

Bloch N., Szmyt Z. (2024) Nomadland. Miejsca zbiorowego zakwaterowania osób uchodźczych z Ukrainy w Wielkopolsce a procesy integracyjne. Poznań: Centrum Badań Migracyjnych UAM.

Boichuk N. (2023) Educational Migration Trends Review in Poland (with Particular Emphasis on the Immigration of Ukrainian Youth). "Studia Migracyjne–Przegląd Polonijny", no. 1(187), pp. 141–162.

Cudzoziemcy… (2023) Raport: "Cudzoziemcy na uczelniach w Polsce" został przygotowany przez ekspertki i ekspertów z Ośrodka Przetwarzania Informacji (OPI) na zlecenie Ministerstwa Edukacji i Nauki (MEiN). Retrieved from: https://radon.nauka.gov.pl/an alizy/cudzoziemcy-na- uczelniach-w-Polsce-2022 (accessed 14.02.2024).

Czerniejewska I. (2016) Uchodźcy – charakterystyka społeczno-kulturowa w kontekście imigracji do Polski. In: Schmidt J., Niedźwiedzki D. (eds.), Społeczno-kulturowa identyfikacja cudzoziemców. Raporty i ekspertyzy. Poznań: Wydawnictwo Naukowe UAM, pp. 603–680.

Geryk M. (2011) Uczelnie niepubliczne – dzieci gorszego Boga? Dlaczego fundusze europejskie nierówno wspierają polskie uczelnie? "Nauka i Szkolnictwo Wyższe", no 2 (38), pp. 139–150.

Herzfeld M. (1997) Cultural Intimacy Social Poetics and the Real Life of States, Societies, and Institutions. New York, London: Routledge.

Jarosz S., Klaus W. (eds.) (2023) Polska szkoła pomagania. Przyjęcie osób uchodźczych z Ukrainy w Polsce w 2022 roku. Warszawa: Konsorcjum Migracyjne, Ośrodek Badań nad Migracjami Uniwersytetu Warszawskiego, Centrum Badań Migracyjnych UAM.

Levchuk P. (2020) Trójjęzyczność ukraińsko-rosyjsko-polska w Ukraińców niepolskiego pochodzenia. Kraków: Księgarnia Akademicka.

Mirowska-Łoskot U. (2021) Polskie uczelnie tylko dla… obcokrajowców. "Dziennik Gazeta Prawna" 6.01.

Stachowicz J. (2013) Niż demograficzny w szkolnictwie wyższym–konsekwencje i proponowane sposoby przeciwdziałania niekorzystnym tendencjom J Stachowicz Pedagogika Szkoły Wyższej, no.13, pp. 63–74.

Williams A. (2007) Listen to me, learn with me: International migration and knowledge. "British Journal of Industrial Relations" 45(2), pp. 361–382.

Wimmer A. (2007) How (not) to think about ethnicity in immigrant societies: A boundary making perspective. Compas Working Papers 07-44. Oxford: Centre on Migration, Policy and Society.

Karol Krzyżosiak (University of Gdańsk)

Polish with TikTok. Online forms of language acquisition among Ukrainian learners of Polish. A case study in netnolinguistics[1]

Abstract

This study explores selected TikTok accounts focused on teaching Polish language and culture to Ukrainians, analyzing their content and underlying assumptions. Utilizing netnolinguistics, a novel approach tailored for this research, we investigate the Polish virtual glottosphere within one of the most successful recent applications. Our goal is to identify and conceptualize the structure and features of learning materials crafted by Ukrainian TikTokers teaching and practicing Polish.

Introduction

Among the most important challenges faced by Ukrainians who have reached Poland after the beginning of Russian invasion is overcoming the language barrier in order to satisfy the basic needs, adapt to the new environment and assure social mobility. Polish and Ukrainian, although closely related, are not mutually understandable: while intercomprehension seems to help learners of both languages, studies also emphasize the influence of negative transfer on generating errors (Saturno 2023). Thus, the need for social adaptation and ac-culturation creates a significant demand for means of learning Polish as a foreign language (PFL) to which the supply is delivered with a surprising efficiency by Ukrainians themselves. Indeed, one can observe the emergence of rich variety of content creators who offer tuition online by means of social media and mobile applications. Those self-made tutors are mostly people with migrant experience who had come to Poland before the war started. Even though many of the creators do not have linguistic or didactic background, their lessons cover a vast variety of topics, providing lexical, phonetic and cultural explanations in a most accessible manner. TikTok is here the leading medium for such purposes. The application is

1 This article is the result of research conducted as part of the project titled "Mapping new agents and trends in teaching Polish as a foreign language among Ukrainian migrants in Poland", implemented under the NAWA Intervention Grant BPN/GIN/2022/1/00088.

ubiquitous and highly immersive, and its features are explored by the users not only in search of sheer entertainment, but also of educational content. Considering the platform's significance for millions of young individuals globally, TikTok has become a subject of growing interest among social scientists. In recent years researchers have progressively employed TikTok as a means to examine the cultural, social, and political attitudes and experiences of the youth (Miltsov 2022). However, there is no systematic research concerning the rich offer of materials for PFL learning that exists on TikTok. This phenomenon enables thousands of Ukrainians to practice Polish and explore the culture through videos crafted by compatriots with more extensive migrant experience and deeper knowledge of the language and culture.

This study is conceived as a multi-perspective research (Paltridge 2020) and it focuses on the creation and distribution of learning materials, cultural content and live lessons in Polish virtual glottosphere (Krzyżosiak 2024) via TikTok. Within the scope of this analysis 10 selected accounts will be analyzed following the criteria of form and function. The analysis will be complemented by three semi-structured interviews with the creators. The overarching methodological framework of this research is *netnolinguistics* – a new concept that was proposed as part of the ongoing NAWA intervention grant, titled *Mapping new agents and trends in teaching Polish as a foreign language among Ukrainian immigrants in Poland* (Krzyżosiak 2024). Netnolinguistics, derived from netnography (Kozinets 2020), is a transdisciplinary (Kita 2012) field studying linguistic phenomena in online contexts, combining linguistics, ethnography, and internet studies. It explores sociolinguistic patterns, communication practices, and psycholinguistic processes in online spaces, highlighting the interplay of online culture, identity construction, and language use. Additionally, it emphasizes the role of both human and non-human agents, including devices and applications, employing actor-network theory (Latour 2005) and a posthumanist perspective to analyze interactions and discursive strategies in digital contexts for a deeper understanding of language, society, and technology in the digital age (Deleuze & Guattari 1987). By means of this transdisciplinary approach, we attempt to reconstruct and conceptualize the underlying frames, thought-patterns, beliefs, subjective theories and convictions that lend structure to the content of analyzed materials, motivate the prioritization of certain aspects over others, and determine the choice of methods, strategies and heuristics applied by creators (White 2008). This, in turn, should contribute to elaborating knowledge and strategies enabling us to create an educational environment that is more inclusive and adapted to the needs of modern learner with migration experience (Gębal et al. 2018).

Research methods and key concepts

In order to recognize and categorize the sociolinguistic patterns of common beliefs, themes and subjective theories that inform given formal choices, strategies and practices of content creation, we apply frame analysis. Frames are socially constructed structures of experience that enable interaction in social situations and their interpretation (Goffman 1986). In the context of this study, the analysis involves examining the language, communication patterns, and scenarios of selected TikTok videos. Content analysis also entails systematically evaluating and categorizing given materials into frames, formats, and strategies employed by TikTok teachers, helping identify recurring themes, trends, and instructional approaches.

As far as framing of the content is concerned, we propose four operational definitions:
- Narration
- Pronunciation-oriented practice
- Scenes (dialogues)
- Translation (verbal or audio-visual)

Narration is to be understood here as a continuous discourse in target language involving problem explanation (i.e. idiomatic expressions), storytelling (i.e. relating an event), response to viewers' questions (i.e. "Why did you decide to learn Polish?") or reflection (i.e. the meaning of the word *szczęście* – Polish word for "happiness"). This kind of content provides the most complex input in form of natural utterances. It includes at once grammatical input, rich vocabulary and pronunciation practice. It is usually performed by the most advanced speakers.

Pronunciation-oriented practice consists on presentation of single words, as well as entire expressions with the focus on correct speaking. This strategy often includes tongue-twisters or short poems based on voice instrumentation and other literary devices exploiting pronunciation difficulties and sound similarities.

Scenes consist on short roleplay interactions between two or more personae with the camera focusing on the one that is speaking. Scenes usually relate humorous interactions between Ukrainians and Poles, highlighting common mistakes and misunderstandings due to negative transfer. Note that thanks to TikTok editing tools enabling cuts, as well as various filters and effects, the roleplay scenes can be realized by just one person playing all the roles, which is quite often the case.

Translation is the most basic form of content offering single expressions or shortlists of words in both languages. It is most often found in two forms: verbal only or audiovisual. The first one consists on written and spoken input, while the latter adds image to the words.

This typology should not be considered as definitive, as it only presents a general grasp on the observed tendencies and does not exhaust all the possible forms of content. The above-mentioned categories will be included in the analysis as a preliminary reconnaissance to get an idea of the broader trend. The study will also consider available numerical data, such as followers and likes, as well as the status of the account (i. e. private, NGO etc.) and dominant language used in videos. After describing and categorizing data, selected videos will be discussed in form of case studies.

Finally, three semi-structured interviews with content creators will be discussed in order to enable the triangulation of analyzed material. The interviews were held in the framework of interpretive paradigm in cultural anthropology, based on the propositions of linguistic anthropology (Ahearn 2020). The primary epistemological foundation of this qualitative method is constructivism, where language serves as the tool of the study and meaning is its subject matter (Buliński 2014). In this approach, the investigator acts as a translator and interpreter, while the Other becomes a partner and interlocutor (ibid.).

Challenges

During twelve months the researcher has been following 10 TikTok accounts led by Ukrainians speaking Polish or creating consistent videos concerned with Polish tuition. These two criteria: Ukrainian origin of the creator and Polish-speaking orientation of the account, as simple as they might seem, make such accounts difficult to trace. The basic method to start with is using keywords like "Polish language" ("język polski") or "learning Polish" ("nauka polskiego"). It is worth mentioning that Ukrainians do not use English as commonly as their Polish neighbors and their tags are mostly in Ukrainian or Polish. Moreover, PFL is obviously not an exclusive domain of Ukrainians: apart from Polish teachers, there are also speakers from Belarus, Russia and other Slavic countries, as well as immigrants from Western Europe who create content in Polish. Finally, user's origin is rarely traceable by keywords. If the country of origin is displayed at all, it is mostly by the use of an icon with the flag in the bio.

For similar reasons it is difficult to estimate the *population*, which is in this context the overall number of TikTok accounts on which Ukrainians speak or teach Polish. The diverse strategies of tagging do not "feed" the algorithm with unified data. Hence the need for manual verification by using selected hashtags and checking the number of publications with given keywords.

Another difficulty concerns the availability of the creators for interviews. Reaching out to the users is a limited strategy for obvious personal reasons: not everyone wishes to engage with a stranger writing from a private account, in spite of most polite requests with due explanations. The lack of response from the part of most popular creators can also be explained by the traffic on their accounts and the lack of time to engage with all the followers sending private messages. Despite these obstacles, three semi-structured interviews were realized within the scope of this study, and their results are presented in the last part of this analysis.

Numeric data and the characteristics of the accounts

The first step of research consists on collecting and organizing the available data concerning the analyzed content, and relevant to the study: number of followers and number of likes. Although TikTok does not reveal much of its numeric data regarding users, this basic information seems to tell just enough about the popularity of the researched materials.

The sample consists of 10 accounts selected on the basis of content involved with Polish language created by a user of Ukrainian origin. This means that in collecting the sample, the emphasis on popularity was only loosely considered. Thus, the possible diversity in popularity of the accounts is unintentional and should be understood as occurring naturally in the process of selection. Furthermore, the inclusion of possible outliers (extreme values) can offer a unique perspective on the variability in content creation and audience engagement.

The data in question is particularly dynamic: the numbers change constantly and by the time this paper is published, the information will no longer be up to date. It seems nevertheless useful to give the reader a notion about the dimensions of the phenomenon precisely at the time of this study being conducted.

The table below presents the collected data in random order, including the discrete numeric data (followers and likes) and basic qualitative data concerning status, content type and dominant language within each account. Note that this representation does not include occasional live streams, as it can be assumed that almost every successful TikToker conducts them with more or less frequency.

Name	Followers	Likes	Status	Content type	Dominant language
User 1	26 K	675 K	Private	Translation, narration, pronunciation	PL&UKR
User 2	132 K	1.5 M	Private	Translation, narration, pronunciation	UKR
User 3	275	6 K	NGO	Narration, scenes	PL

(Continued)

Name	Followers	Likes	Status	Content type	Dominant language
User 4	22 K	97 K	Private	Audio-visual translation, scenes	PL&UKR
User 5	90 K	1.5 M	Private	Audio-visual translation, scenes	PL&UKR
User 6	87 K	2.1 M	Private	Narration, audio-visual translation, scenes	PL&UKR
User 7	28 K	192 K	Private	Narration	PL
User 8	22 K	121 K	NGO	Scenes, narration	PL
User 9	220 K	5.8 M	Self-employment	Scenes, translation	PL
User 10	45 K	303 K	Self-employment	Narration, translation	PL&UKR

The noticeable outlier value of 275 followers in case of User 3 can be explained by the local character of the NGO they represent and the fact that PFL tuition is not its' main activity. The NGO in question, Migrant Info Point in Poznań, states on its' website that the principal aim of their activity is to support people and families coming to Poznań in adapting to new conditions, as well as providing comprehensive assistance. Thence, language tuition on TikTok should be considered as an additional activity. However, one of my interviewees provides a more insightful information on the matter, which will be discussed later.

In order to clean the dataset and avoid the result being skewed, the above-mentioned outlier is not considered in calculating the average number of followers and likes. This means that the average number of followers in our sample is 75 K within the range of 22K to 220K (range=198K), with the median of 45 K. As for likes, within the range of 97K to 5.8M (range≈5.7M), the average number is 1.4 M and the median 675 K.

What cannot be concluded from the table above, but what is nevertheless confirmed by observation, the majority of accounts in question are led by female creators. During this observation, the researcher only encountered three accounts led by male creators, one of which shall be discussed in case study.

As said earlier, the presented data are intended to show approximately the scale of the phenomenon in question. However, it also provides us with a preliminary insight into tendencies concerning some of the most common forms of framing the content. Above all, it indicates the significant role of private agents, either amateurs or self-employed tutors, in the distribution of PFL content. It also shows that within the diversity of available content there are some easily distinguishable trends of framing the video depending on the particular learning objective. It can finally be safely assumed that the majority of the observed accounts favor eclectic methods.

It has to be kept in mind that the results are indicative: the dominant content type does not exclude other strategies employed by a given user, nor the sporadic videos unrelated to language learning. The same applies to the dominant language: for instance, Users 3, 7, 8 and 9 use Polish quite exclusively, while some of the translation-oriented accounts tend to publish videos almost exclusively in Ukrainian, using Polish only to present a given word or expression. Most basic training tends to be presented predominantly in Ukrainian, whereas the most linguistically advanced content is created predominantly in Polish and tends to be framed in form of scenes and narration.

It is worth noting, that some of the creators also regularly provide live lessons and consultations thanks to streaming option on TikTok. Some of them also include fragments of their private online lessons in their videos, where learner's voice can be heard. One can assume that on such occasions the creators have their clients' permissions to use the parts of their lessons as promoting materials for their teaching activity.

Case studies

The following case studies are based on the selected videos from three different users. It is worth mentioning, however, that throughout this study, non-participant observations were also undertaken during live stream lessons involving users from both within and outside the sample analyzed in this paper. It needs to be explained that live-streaming time and frequency are highly dependent of creator's availability and personal preferences, which makes them difficult to monitor systematically. Many of those lessons provide basic level speaking and reading practice through examples, gap-filling and translation, which can be associated with the classical grammar-translation method (Patel & Jain 2008). This "traditional" approach to language tuition reflects some of the predominant concepts in Ukrainian culture of education, which are also familiar for most Polish learners: both teachers and learners tend to internalize the models and theories of language learning utilized and propagated in public schools (Krzyżosiak 2024).

User 1, who also publishes fragments of her lessons in one-minute videos, offers a more modern, functional approach. She provides instruction in both one-on-one sessions and small group settings. When working with beginners, User 1 employs Ukrainian, but she predominantly communicates in Polish with more advanced students. She employs individual, learner-oriented techniques with emphasis on communication. This can be seen in the choice of materials adapted to learner's personal preferences, as in the case of teaching colors on the basis of cartoon *My little pony* which was the learner's favorite.

The emphasis on variation also seems to be an important aspect of User 1's subjective teaching theory. Greeting the learners with *hej, hejka, siema, siemanko*, she introduces a variety of most common informal greetings. Similarily, her video of merely 15 seconds offers different variants of the expression *myślę, że* ("I think that"), such as: *moim zdaniem* ("in my opinion"), *uważam, że* ("I ponder that"), *według mnie* ("according to me"), *jestem przekonana* ("I am convinced")[2]. Presentation of different variants of expressions and synonyms is a common practice among the observed creators, especially those providing a more basic, beginner-oriented instruction.

User 5 often frames her content as a traditional classroom situation. The creator plays the role of a Polish teacher greeting her students and presenting a given topic. However, there is always a plot-twist in the presented scene. A frequent storytelling device consists on presenting a grammatical rule to a student (played by the same person), who acquires it with ease only to discover towards the end of the video that there is a significant exception to the rule.

One such scenario occurs in the video dedicated to *biernik* – Polish accusative case. In the beginning, the topic is present as a "very simple" one. The teacher presents traditional auxiliary questions intended to help the learner in declination of the nouns and adjectives by cases: *kogo? co? (widzę)* meaning "who or what (I see)". Then the teacher proceeds to explain the concept of animate and inanimate masculine forms. If a noun is animate, the noun takes the ending *-a*, and the adjective takes the ending *-ego*, as in:

Nominative: *starszy brat* – Accusative *Mam starszego brata*
("older brother" – "I have an older brother")

N. *duży pies* – Acc. *Mam dużego psa*
("big dog" – "I have a big dog")

The general rule is that inanimate masculine objects do not vary in Polish accusative, as in:

N. *Wolny czas* – Acc. *Mam wolny czas*
("free time" – "I have free time")

N *Niebieski sweter* – Acc. *Kupiłam niebieski sweter*
("blue sweater" – "I bought a blue sweater")

The student is glad that they do not need to learn any additional endings and proceeds to decline the nouns and adjectives with ease and satisfaction. However, in the turning point of the video, right after telling the student to write down the

---

2 These are ethnographic, "literal" translations of most common Polish expressions and should not be considered as their equivalents.

presented rules, the teacher turns to somebody out of frame to show them their new iPhone:

Zobacz, dostałam na urodziny nowego iPhone'a.
("Look, I got a new iPhone on my birthday")

The camera instantly focuses on the learner's face, showing confusion and disbelief: they were told that inanimate masculine objects do not take any endings in Polish accusative. And yet the new iPhone behaves as if it was alive. "But iPhone is not alive", says the learner in Polish. "Well, iPhone is not alive, but you need to transform the brand name", replies the teacher giving examples of different brands:

Mam iPhone'a, mam Samsunga... no i Mercedesa... też bym chciała mieć.
("I have an iPhone, a Samsung... and a Mercedes... I'd like to have one too")

Thus, the learner needs to accept the peculiar exception. But that is not all. Having explained the nuance as if it were the most obvious thing in the world, the teacher asks the entire class: *Kto chce po lekcji zagrać w tenisa?* ("Who wants to play tennis after the lesson?"). Once again, the inanimate word *tenis* behaves like animate masculine nouns. Utterly confused, the learner states with resignation: *polska język, łatwa język* ("Polish language, simple language"), a common phrase rendered ironically erratic by adding feminine endings to the adjectives referring to a masculine noun. The whole video lasts 2 minutes and 9 seconds.

User 9 is the most popular TikToker from our sample. A male creator, he provides humoristic educational content on TikTok, as well as on Instagram. He also runs his own educational business. User 9 publishes videos in form of short scenes and translations of words and expressions of everyday use. As far as humor is concerned, this creator does not restrain from colloquial language, offering deep cultural insights into some of the most common obscenities of Polish language. One of some more public-appropriate examples are popular expressions, such as *nie wciskaj nosa w nieswoje sprawy* ("Don't stick your nose into matters that aren't yours"), or *piździ, pizga* or *piździawa*, which are colloquial terms describing cold weather, and derived from the word *pizda* ("cunt").

In his roleplay scenes, the creator plays both male and female characters, often involved in romantic relationships. Many of such videos present qui pro quos arising from double entendre, as in telephone exchange between partners in which the woman confuses eating neighbor's "seeds" and "semen" – *nasiona* (plural) and *nasienie* (singular).

In other cases, different situations display multiple uses of the same colloquial word. On such example is the common use of the expression *spoko* – short for *spokojnie* ("take it easy"). In this 30 second video the creator plays as many as 8 roles in 4 separate dialogues, in which *spoko* is the answer to different questions:

Between friends:
No i co, jak ten nowy kolega?
("So, how's the new colleague?")

On the construction site:
Ej, Michał, podejdziesz tutaj?
("Hey, Michał, will you come here?")

Between the boss and the employee:
Przepraszam, no ale jest pan zwolniony.
("I am sorry, but you are fired")

About food:
No i jak, smakuje?
("So, do you like it?")

One particular video seems to stand out as a call for inclusive treatment from native speakers and, at the same time, a commercial for user's own services. Two personae are involved in the scene: a Ukrainian who pronounces Polish expression with difficulty and a "policeman of Polish language". Although the sentences uttered by the Ukrainian were quite understandable, the law officer stops the "offender" saying "you again", and proceeds to correct his imperfection in a very precise manner. He then asks the delinquent what he should do with him, to which the repentant Ukrainian replies: "Understand. And forgive". The policeman then responds: "for this offense you will receive... a discount on Polish language courses".

Interviews

The final part of the study is the reconstruction of three semi-structured interviews, two of which were led by means of video calls on Instagram and Messenger and one in written form via messaging feature built-in on TikTok.

In the interviews, the following questions were addressed:
1. What is the character of a given material? (language tuition, entertainment, acculturation, sharing migrant knowledge)
2. What is the structure of the analyzed content?
3. What are the topics and scenarios?
4. What is the role of humor in the creation of learning materials?
5. What are implicit beliefs and subjective theories underlying the materials?

User 1

The interview with User 1 was conducted in a written form. The creator has been learning Polish for 6 years now, but she does not currently live in Poland. Her adventure with Polish started during the second year of her studies of Ukrainian philology at Petro Mohyla Black Sea State University in Mykolaiv. Polish, however was not her first choice as an additional Slavic language. In fact, she had primarily wanted to study Bulgarian – it was the majority of her group who decided otherwise. And yet, in hindsight, User 1 considers herself lucky, when she recalls her classes with a Polish lecturer appointed by NAWA, who also conducted Polish exams in Mykolaiv. The course lasting around 2 years was based on the use of one of the most popular textbooks for Polish, *Krok po kroku* ("Step by step") (I. Stempek; A. Stelmach; S. Dawidek; A. Szymkiewicz, 2010). User 1 recalls that her group consisted only of girls. She states that their level of speaking was "weak" (*słaby*), which means "far from satisfactory". She points to lack of practice, time and motivation as the main reasons.

> Everything changed when I started taking part in NAWA summer school. These are 3–4-week intensive Polish language and culture courses. In 2018 I was at the University of Wrocław, in 2019 in Siedlce. Then the quarantine started, so the courses were held remotely. During this period, I participated in courses from the University of Warsaw and the University of Silesia. These courses changed my life, because when I first came to Poland, I started practicing more and talking to people from different countries IN POLISH.
> So, when I came home I was inspired.
> Now I have language arts lessons with a Polish woman. I want to talk, write, speak better. I have been teaching beginners for almost 4 years. However, I know that I lack vocabulary and practice because I do not live in Poland. I dream that I will soon pass the C1 Polish exam. I would really like to

When asked about most common difficulties, User 1 mentions vocabulary and grammar ("I hate the genitive case!"). As a solution, she tries to watch Polish YouTube and television every day. She also decided to buy books in Polish to "keep in touch" with the language. These strategies highlight the intuitive understanding of the importance of what Stephen Krashen would call a "comprehensible input" (Krashen 1982) in language acquisition.

Close affinity between Polish and Ukrainian might also be seen as a problem. User 1 points especially at the negative transfer as source of difficulties for more advanced speakers:

> The Ukrainian language and the Polish language are very similar, and this has a positive effect only at the beginning. It is often the case that Ukrainians understand better and learn new words faster than others. However, the higher the level, the worse it is for Ukrainians, because there are many language traps, the so-called negative transfer.

Negative transfer is the most common difficulty observed among Ukrainians learning Polish, not only by teachers, but also by themselves (Krawczuk 2009, 2013; Czebanenko 2017; Czapla 2020). This means that the awareness of the existence of negative transfer is strongly internalized and considered as a nuisance to communication. When asked if she feels anxious, judged or ashamed when using Polish, she responds: "Yes of course, and I guess I can never get rid of that feeling. I still make mistakes, I don't have perfect pronunciation, etc. After all, I'm a foreigner, not Polish I try to be a good teacher for my students. I'm still learning and learning Polish". Despite the fact that she has been teaching beginners for over 4 years now, she still feels insecure about her speaking competence and lack of vocabulary. She dreams of passing C1 one exam sometime soon.

User 3

The next interviewee, User 3, represents a very particular case of a person of Polish origin brought up in Ukraine who needed to learn Polish as her mother tongue at the age of twelve. The interview took place via Messenger and lasted for over an hour.

Given the natural bilingualism of children growing up in Ukraine, as they learn both Ukrainian and Russian at school, User 3 had to learn the language of her parents as her third language. Her background includes high school education, volunteer work, and a burgeoning interest in ethnolinguistics. She aspires to become a polyglot linguist, seamlessly integrating her educational pursuits with income-generating activities. Born in Ukraine, she resided there until the age of 16 before relocating to Poland in 2017/2018. Her language acquisition journey commenced with courses in Kyiv, where initial motivation was lacking. Recognizing the importance of structured learning, she immersed herself in Polish by listening to spoken language, reading literary works such as *The Little Prince*, children's stories, and songs. After a two-year period, proficiency increased, though grammatical challenges persisted.

In her reflection on applied teaching methods, User 3 explored linguistic nuances, particularly homonyms or "false friends", exemplified by distinctions like *dywan* (pol. "carpet") and *dywan* (ukr. "couch"). She also emphasised overcoming the apprehension associated with speaking, advocating an early initiation of conversational practice for accelerated language proficiency. Contextual vocabulary was addressed, referencing the Ilya Frank method, involving literature translations, simultaneous text readings, and shadowing.

Interestingly, the interviewee conceptualized language learning as a pyramid, prioritizing vocabulary, speaking, and grammar. Regarding teaching techniques and the use of technology, she emphasized engaging presentations utilizing tools like Canva and slideshows. The significance of visual aesthetics, camera work, and video editing in content creation was discussed to create an engaging learning environment. Despite setting high standards for correctness, the interviewee encouraged a continuous pursuit of improvement.

User 7

The interview with User 7 was conducted via video call on Instagram. Primarily, the interviewee was presented with some general information concerning the research project and the character of interviews. After expressing interest in participating in the research, User 7 asked a few questions concerning the project and my credentials, she also asked if she could read some of my papers, which I sent her via email. After a short exchange of availabilities, as we were both unable to find a convenient time slot, we decided to catch up on a call immediately, in spite of late hour.

The interview lasted around 20 minutes. The person does not primarily consider her TikTok activity as teaching, even though she also teaches Polish professionally in the physical space. On TikTok, however, she claims to be merely "sharing her passion" for Polish language. Yet her face is one of the first images to appear when one types "język polski" (Polish language) in TikToks search engine. Being 29 years old, she had spent 9 years in Poland and now lives in Wrocław.

A specific type of learner, User 7 describes herself as being unconditionally passionate about Polish language. In the background of most of her videos one can here Chopin's nocturne no 2., which clearly underscores the Polish character of the content, but at the same tame creates a grotesque atmosphere that merges humorous observations with deep thoughts. Indeed, despite reflexive and often quite serious character of her videos, User 7 points that humor is essential in creating an engaging content.

She mentions prof. Jerzy Bralczyk, a famous Polish linguist, as the main source of inspiration for practice. One of her preferred strategies of learning was transcribing Bralczyk's lectures. This also seems to be an important influence on her content where she often presents rare Polish words and discusses their origins. In one of her videos, she ponders upon the correspondence between the sound of some Polish words and their meanings. She evokes the words *krótki* ("short") and *długi* ("long"), as well as *trzeszczenie* ("crackle"), *trzask* ("crack") and *strzał* ("shot").

Highly advanced and aiming at nearly "native" level of fluency, this type of content seems to serve as a learning practice for the user herself. While for the viewer it might certainly constitute a valuable input, for the creator it is at once

speaking and vocabulary exercise. This fact seems to blur the traditional linguistic distinctions between users, learners and teachers of a given language.

Conclusion

One of the most important takeaways from the analysis of the videos made by
Ukrainian speakers of Polish on TikTok is that content creation merges systematic practice on the part of the creator with offering the viewers a comprehensive didactic input. In other words, we can watch people learn almost in real
time. Thus, the concepts of "learning" and "teaching" become at times blurry and
problematic, as many of the creators seem to quite intuitively bring to life the
ancient maxim *dum docemus, discimus.* Whether narrating events and experiences, practicing pronunciation, playing scenes or just presenting vocabulary
through translation, the creators publicly organize and consolidate their own
knowledge and skills while at the same time sharing their progress, observations
and migrant knowledge with others. This highlights the importance of self-
monitoring and systematic auto-evaluation in learning process. One could
plausibly argue that content creation in general could be a purposeful strategy
worth applying in formal education, bearing in mind that publishing does not
have to be a compulsory part of such practice.

Learning language on TikTok not only involves watching others learn, but also
immersing oneself into first-hand cultural context presented by a compatriot – a
genuine gatekeeper who imparts proven practices, keywords and patterns of
linguistic behavior forming the linguistic inventory of migrant knowledge. This
mediation in migrant experience tends to blur the classical distinction between
learning and acquisition as well as the boundaries between a foreign and a second
language. Indeed, one can observe that the most frequent content offers simple
translations of useful words and expressions or scenes from everyday life reflecting practical situations immersing the viewer in a common migrant experience. On one hand, this indicates practice-oriented learning that favors communicational skills and envisions language first and foremost as an adaptational
tool. On the other hand, it shows a significant role of storytelling as heuristic
device. The most successful videos present a story with a proper exposition,
suspense and denouement. Storytelling enhances immersion and encourages
engagement. It can be argued that as a heuristic it helps incorporate new
knowledge in a structured manner instead of catalogizing separate terms and
concepts. Furthermore, as an integral component in majority of cases, humor
was identified as a potent instructional tool, providing memorable heuristics,
engaging viewer's interest and facilitating the identification of errors while
sustaining a light-hearted atmosphere. More than a mere addition to the in-

formative content, it constitutes its' main feature structuring the micro-stories in the way that permits to achieve the desired comic effect and engaging storytelling.

Technology also provides new ways of communication and interaction. The live streaming option available on TikTik after reaching 1000 followers, enables not only two-way exchange between active actors, but also what theory of communication calls "an omnidirectional diachronic process of meaning development", in which "interaction is seen as a dynamic interplay between actors in their roles as senders and receivers" (van Ruler 2018). The teaching and learning process become a public event, available for anyone. This, in turn, makes it an opportunity for the creator to consolidate their community and extend their reach. The followers can simply watch the stream or interact with the creator via chat, but they can also support them with gifts if they wish. However, for the majority of viewers the streams, as well as the videos, are available for free. This leads to the conclusion that, above all, the study of the Ukrainian Polish-speaking glottosphere on TikTok emphasizes the fusion of passion, creativity, and pedagogy among individuals involved in a bottom-up initiative to disseminate the knowledge of Polish as a gateway language for thousands of migrants and refugees.

Bibliography

Ahearn Laura N. (2017) Living Language – An Introduction to Linguistic Anthropology. Wiley Blackwell, Oxford.

Buliński T. (2014) Ruchoma wiedza terenowa. Perspektywa antropologii procesualnej. Zeszyty Etnologii Wrocławskiej nr 2014/2(21).

Czapla A. (2020) Błędy leksykalne Ukraińców uczących się języka polskiego w Polsce. "Linguodidactica" XXIV, DOI: 10.15290/lingdid.2020.24.03.

Czebanenko, A. (2017) Typowe błędy i trudności językowe pojawiające się w trakcie nauczania Ukraińców języka polskiego jako obcego. Annales Universitatis Paedagogicae Cracoviensis. Studia Ad Didacticam Litterarum Polonarum Et Linguae Polonae Pertinentia, 7(223), pp. 31–37. https://didactica.up.krakow.pl/article/view/3858.

Deleuze G., Guattari F. (1987) A Thousand Plateaus: Capitalism and Schizophrenia. University of Minnesota Press.

Duff P. (2007) Case study research in applied linguistics. Lawrence Erlbaum Associates, New York.

Fazilatfar (et al.) (2014) Learners' Belief Changes about Language Learning. International Journal of English Language Education.

Friedman R., George A. (eds.) (2022) Online Language Teaching in Diverse Contexts. Cambridge Scholars Publishing, Newcastle.

Gębal P.E. et al. (2018) Edukacja wobec migracji: konteksty glottodydaktyczne i pedagogiczne. Księgarnia Akademicka, Kraków.

Goffman E. (1986) Frame analysis. An essay on the organization of experience. Northeastern University Press, Boston.

Kita, M. (2012) Razem: konsiliencja, interdyscyplinarność, transdyscyplinarność. W: M. Kita, M. Ślawska (red.), "Transdyscyplinarność badań nad komunikacją medialną. T. 1, Stan wiedzy i postulaty badawcze". Wydawnictwo Uniwersytetu Śląskiego, Katowice.

Kozinets R. (2020) Netnography: The Essential Guide to Qualitative Social Media Research. Sage Publications Ltd, London.

Krashen S. (1982) Principles and Practice in Second Language Acquisition. Pergamon Press Inc.

Krzyżosiak K. (2014) Learning Beliefs and Strategies Among Ukrainian Polish Speakers in the Face of War in Ukraine. An insight from linguistic anthropology. In: Gębal P.E., Janowska I. (red.), Theory and Practice of Polish Language Teaching. New Methodological Concepts. Göttingen: Vandenhoeck & Ruprecht Verlage (V&R unipress).

Latour B. (2005) Reassembling the Social: An Introduction to Actor-Network-Theory. Oxford UP, Oxford.

Miltsov, A. (n.d.) Researching TikTok: Themes, methods, and future directions. In The SAGE Handbook of Social Media Research Methods, 2nd Edition, edited by A. Quan-Haase, and L. Sloan. SAGE. https://dx.doi.org/10.4135/9781529782943.n46.

Patel M.F., Jain P.M. (2008) English language teaching (methods, tools & techniques). Sunrise Publishers and Distributors, Jaipur.

Paltridge B. (2020) "Multi-perspective research" in: J. McKinley, H. Rose (eds.) The Routledge Handbook of Research Methods in Applied Linguistics. Routledge, New York.

Ruler, Betteke van. (2018) Communication Theory: An Underrated Pillar on Which Strategic Communication Rests. International Journal of Strategic Communication, 12(4), 367–381. DOI: 10.1080/1553118X.2018.1452240.

Saturno J. (2023) Bliskość pomiędzy językami słowiańskimi a integracja uchodźców z Ukrainy w Polsce. Poznańskie Studia Polonistyczne – Seria językoznawcza, vol. 30 (50), nr 1. https://doi.org/10.14746/pspsj.2023.30.1.9.

Stempek, Iwona; Stelmach, Anna; Dawidek Sylwia; Szymkiewicz, Aneta. (2010) Polski. Krok po kroku. Glossa.

White C. (2008) Beliefs and good language learners. Cambridge University Press, Cambridge.

Przemysław E. Gębal (University of Gdańsk)

Towards didactic concepts of differentiation and personalization. Teaching Polish as a second language in the face of the changing linguistic, communication and activity needs of migrating learners (with particular emphasis on Eastern Slavs)

Abstract

The increasing number of citizens of foreign countries staying in Poland naturally affects the organization and implementation of education in our country, both at the school and academic level. It also changes the way in which preparation and professional development are organized and implemented, considering the needs of migrating adults preparing to enter the Polish labor market. The described situation has a direct impact on the teaching of Polish as a second language in the context of migration and on the development of the research space covering learning and teaching Polish as a non-native language. The article presents emerging trends in the substantive and programmatic implementation and organization of Polish language education in the context of migration. It shows further directions of development of individual teaching concepts, locating them in new social, educational and professional contexts.

Introduction. Socio-educational context

According to the report of the Office for Foreigners of February 24, 2023, approximately 1 million Ukrainian citizens, mainly women and children, benefit from temporary protection in Poland. A total of 1.4 million people have valid residence permits in the country[1]. In turn, the latest available report from June 29, 2022 regarding Belarusian citizens indicates that they are the second most numerously represented group of foreigners in Poland[2]. A significant increase in the scale of migration in this case has been noticeable since August 2020. After Ukraine and Belarus, among foreigners legally residing in Poland there are citizens of Georgia[3], Germany and Russia.

The increasing number of citizens of foreign countries residing in Poland naturally affects the organization and implementation of education in our

---

1 https://www.gov.pl/web/udsc/obywatele-ukrainy-w-polsce-aktualne-dane-migracyjne2 (12.12.2023).

2 https://www.gov.pl/web/udsc/obywatele-bialorusi-w-polsce-raport2 (12.12.2023).

3 https://www.gov.pl/web/udsc/obywatele-gruzji-w-polsce--raport (12.12.2023).

country, both at the school and academic level, as well as outside it, including classes for adults entering or preparing to enter the labor market. The described situation also has a direct impact on the teaching of Polish as a second language in the context of migration and on the development of the research space covering learning and teaching Polish as a non-native language.

The texts presented in the volume review in a quite transparent way the existing concepts of teaching Polish as a non-native language. They combine a number of psycholinguistic and didactic considerations, relating them to both institutionalized language education and out-of-school and non-academic formats of organizing and implementing Polish language education. They also indicate the need for greater interest in the teaching of Polish as a foreign and second language in the group of Eastern Slavs, who constitute a specific group of people learning our language as a foreign and second language from the perspective of psycholinguistics and teaching. At the same time, they revise the teaching and methodological concepts and formats of currently implemented language courses for adults, mainly for Ukrainians and Belarusians, as well as the implemented teaching programs and the increasing number of textbooks and other teaching materials prepared for this group of recipients. They also draw attention to the need to carry out further psycholinguistic and glottodidactic research devoted to non-formalized educational activities, which in a specific way also penetrate the everyday practice of institutionalized Polish language education, changing and modifying the ways of its organization, implementation and evaluation.

Polish language glottodidactics and concepts of teaching Polish as a non-native language at the threshold of the third decade of the 21st century

The term Polish language glottodidactics, defined by Władysław Miodunka in 2016, treats it as a field of humanities dealing with the study of the process of teaching and learning Polish as a foreign and second language (Miodunka 2016: 54). The author of the cited definition supplements it with a clearly expressed belief in the connection and mutual determination of teaching and learning processes, ultimately leading to an increase in the effectiveness of both processes. They constitute equal, complementary spaces for empirical investigations and theoretical reflections in contemporary Polish language glottodidactics (see ibid.). The scientific glottodidactic activity in the field of teaching Polish as a non-native language has been carried out since the late 1960s (see Lewandowski 1979), although the first empirical projects, which translated into the adopted curriculum solutions, began to be implemented and described in the early 1980s.

In a broader academic perspective, Polish language glottodidactics is part of the glottodidactics developed in Poland since the 1960s in the circles of applied linguists. However, the analysis of these connections and interdependencies reveals a number of complexities and conditions which, on the one hand, resulted from the development of Polish thought in the field of applied linguistics and glottodidactics, and on the other hand, reflected the way of scientific perception of teaching Polish as a foreign language in the circles of Polish teachers and specialists in the field of teaching various foreign languages.

In general terms, Polish language glottodidactics also means the practice of teaching and learning Polish as a foreign language, a second language and a language of inherited (origin), conducted in Poland and abroad based on the conceptual, programmatic and didactic-methodological solutions adopted in a given context (Miodunka 2016 , Gębal and Miodunka 2020). This connection between theory and practice is one of the fundamental assumptions determining the sense of conducting glottodidactic research, expressed in studies modeling glottodidactics as a relatively autonomous scientific field (Grucza 1978, Woźniewicz 1987, Pfeiffer 2001, Dakowska 2010, Gębal 2019).

Finally, in relation to everyday teaching practice, Polish language glottodidactics is a set of assumptions, didactic concepts, as well as program proposals and solutions, trying to answer the question of what, why and how to teach. In order to propose formats of methodological solutions adequate to teaching situations, glottodidactics conducts research on specific language, communication and activity needs among individual groups of learners, formulating learning and teaching goals and educational content, based on their results, along with the criteria for their selection. The texts included in the volume consider the above assumption, collecting new needs of Polish language learners and describing related language learning strategies and ways of including them in the classroom context.

The analysis of most contemporary Polish glottodidactic texts leads to the reflection that most of the teaching concepts currently used focus on two areas of educational impact: on the linguistic and personality development of those learning Polish as a non-native language, related to their acquisition of specific linguistic and non-linguistic competences and skills (Gębal and Miodunka 2020, 2023).

The educational approach described is reflected theoretically, empirically and practically in the discussions and research projects carried out recently. Presenting them in the form of detailed directions that constitute the determinants of contemporary teaching of Polish as a foreign and second language, we should mention the concept of action didactics, intercultural teaching, multilingualism didactics and the autonomy of the language education process and the related reflexivity (ibid.).

Introducing this type of elements into teaching Polish as a foreign and second language is a natural reflection of the changing paradigms of language education in Europe and around the world and the adoption of an increasingly stronger constructivist orientation in language education.

In contrast to the communicative didactics promoted over the years, the currently promoted concept of constructivist action didactics is aimed at undertaking linguistic activities embedded in a social context (cf. CEFR-CV 2003 and CEFR-CV 2018). Contemporary educational theories link their substantive assumptions with theories of action that perceive human activity as searching for and organizing specific means necessary to achieve the assumed goals. The concepts developed in philosophy (D. Davidson) and sociology (M. Weber, E. Durkheim, J. Habermas) associate the will and intention to act with cooperation, thanks to which a relationship is created and the resulting individual feeling of action. The development of language skills assigned to communication-oriented teaching (listening comprehension, reading comprehension, speaking and writing) is extended to four types of language activities, which include: oral and written receptive activities in the field of text comprehension, oral and written productive activities. for the production of texts, oral and written interactive activities for the exchange of information, and oral and written mediation activities in the form of processing existing texts. In everyday educational practice, the action approach is present in the form of didactic tasks and projects oriented towards the real needs of learners. Teaching tasks place activities in specific contexts and situations, creating their meaning and giving them authenticity. The proposed didactic formats place activities carried out in and outside classes within clear task patterns that encourage cooperation and interaction with others, which serves linguistic and personal development.

As part of intercultural teaching, classes in Polish as a foreign language include teaching content and activities showing different, culturally determined points of view. The contribution of Polish culture and the cultures of individual learners to the development of global culture is subjected to critical reflection. The processes of mutual influence of cultures and the specific processes and cultural products resulting from them are also presented to a broader extent. In the methodological dimension, in the intercultural context, open forms of learning and teaching dominate, encouraging learners to personally discover their own culture and that of others, including Poland, with all its regional diversity, and subjecting them to critical self-reflection (cf. Gębal 2010, Nawracka 2020).

In the context of didactics of Polish as a second language, dedicated to learners with migration experience, intercultural teaching was an important element of the development of this area of education, which influenced the currently observed process of its separation from the didactics of Polish as a foreign language.

From the concept of multilingualism teaching to teaching Polish as a foreign language, *intercomprehensive* teaching is most often implemented in classes with Eastern Slavs. The basis for the development of this didactic proposal is the desire to use the natural similarity of Eastern Slavic languages to Polish, which favors the particularly effective development of receptive activities, i. e. understanding of written texts, listening comprehension and audiovisual reception, the improvement of which becomes one of the basic goals of teaching at the beginner level A1 (Saturno and Gębal 2022). However, when it comes to intercomprehension, attention is often paid to its strengthening of the fossilization that occurs in the process of language acquisition and its support for negative transfer. This fact often makes teachers moderately optimistic about actively and fully consciously incorporating this didactic concept into their teaching practice. Hence, the presence of intercomprehensive teaching is still greater in hidden teaching interactions than in curricula and teaching materials.

Reflective learners and teachers are people who take act and are prepared to confront uncertainty, the uniqueness of contexts and situations, and the conflicts of values that often result from them. These are self-aware people who can see the value of problem situations in the development of personal theories (cf. Nawracka 2020).

Reflectivity in the context of learning and teaching foreign languages is supported not only by the level of linguistic competence, but by all communication activities taking place during classes, including those in the dimension of interpersonal relations.

The key element determining autonomous teaching, and even a means of creating an autonomous learner, is the ability to reflect (Wilczyńska 2008). In the context of language education, according to Wilczyńska's assumptions, autonomy is an attitude according to which a given person – learning and/or teaching – that is, a subject who self-actualizes in the educational process and, in responsibility for his or her actions, shapes the learning environment in accordance with his or her own assessment, will and views (ibidem). Autonomy is a kind of flexible cooperation between the learner and the teacher, referring to individually understood effectiveness, economic development and improvement in the field of a foreign language. The teacher can offer help to the learner, in terms of information (indicating elements of knowledge, guiding analogies, etc.), technical (methods, useful procedures), and even therapeutic (support and help in understanding fears or resistances).

In everyday educational practice, the autonomous approach is supported by the implementation of open forms of teaching in the form of didactic projects carried out in groups. The mentioned reflexivity, which determines the development of autonomy, is felt especially in the last phase of project implementation, which also includes their critical self-evaluation carried out by those performing project activities (Gębal 2019).

The outlined didactic concepts, although they serve primarily to individualize the language learning process, are primarily dedicated to group classes, within which it is possible to include a number of group situational contexts that support the development of psychosocial competences. These concepts also assume various types of integration and inclusion activities, which are particularly important from the perspective of conducting Polish as a second language classes in the context of migration. Since contemporary Polish language glottodidactics also opts for the inclusion of various types of media in the language education process, the presented concepts offer a number of specific methodological solutions that enable the implementation of this type of learning and teaching.

New needs, learning strategies and pedagogical challenges. Towards personalizing and differentiating concepts of teaching Polish as a non-native language

With the outbreak of full-scale military conflict in Ukraine in 2022, the demand for Polish as a second language courses at all levels of advancement across a wide spectrum of learner profiles has increased dramatically. It included classes conducted in the format of integration courses for adults known from Western European countries, the aim of which was intensive language learning to support acculturation processes taking place among refugees from war. The implementation of this type of teaching was carried out primarily by local governments and non-governmental organizations, usually financed by state-owned companies and international humanitarian funds.

The lack of existing state formalized curriculum solutions meant that the content of this type of courses was usually conceived ad hoc and referred to the assumptions and levels of language proficiency presented in the Common European Framework of Reference for Languages (CEFR) and the examination requirements of the Polish certification system.

Although a large number of non-governmental organizations filled them with additional content aimed at supplementing classes with content and goals conducive to the development of intercultural competences and psychosocial skills, it is difficult to call them well-thought-out activities integrating refugees from war into the Polish community. Taking into account the fact that there are no standardized curricular, didactic and methodological solutions for this type of language education, it is easy to understand the multitude of additional classes offered and their often unclear pedagogical goals. The educational activities undertaken include personalized classes in the format of group tutoring, supplemented with elements of career counseling (Multicultural Center of the capital city of Warsaw), classes with a component of emotional regulation and stress relief techniques (Warsaw Fundacja Samodzielni od Kuchni [SOK]), classes in the field of intercultural communication and specialized languages (Warsaw's nienudno.pl), or additional cultural modules in the field of European civilization and the history and present of Warsaw (University of Warsaw – Warsaw Cultural Research Center).

The courses usually brought students to the B1 or B2 level according to CEFR, and often also offered courses preparing for passing the certificate exam. Due to the need to quickly learn the language, most of the courses were medium-intensive and intensive, usually ranging from 10 to 25 hours of classes per week. Weekend classes were also conducted. The classes were conducted in stationary, hybrid or remote mode, so that the participants could choose them and adapt them to their real time and organizational possibilities. In most cases, the courses were free of charge, and their participants also received free packages of teaching materials.

All of the above-mentioned units additionally offered educational and improvement activities for teachers of Polish as a second language, whose demand on the educational labor market has increased massively. The short-term forms of training and development for teachers offered include the implementation of content covering, to varying degrees, the concepts and directions of contemporary Polish language education mentioned at the beginning of this text, reinforced with additional content, usually reflecting classes proposed by given centers to complement language learning. In the case of the SOK Foundation, these were psychoeducational classes on supporting emotional regulation in learners, and nienudno.pl offered intercultural workshops and classes on creative planning of classes in selected specialized languages. Considering the high demand for teachers on the labor market, educational activities were, in the first phase, also conducted by students and unqualified teachers of various languages and school subjects. The offer of short-term improvement courses has therefore often become the only possible educational path preparing for employment as a teacher of Polish as a second language. To date, due to the lack of a formal concept of migration policy at the national level, no standardized program assumptions have been developed for integration language courses or education standards for teachers conducting classes within this type of language education format. Since the financing of this type of teaching activities has practically ended recently, the implementation of integration courses is now carried out to a very limited extent, becoming basically a marginal activity. Here and there, the classes offered are extremely popular and registration for starting groups closes soon after they open. The experiences described were probably the most important moment in the history of the development of Polish language glottodi-dactics. The highest rates among learners, substantial interest in professional training for teachers and lectors of Polish as a non-native language, and the growing demand for textbooks and teaching materials have launched a whole range of activities in 2022 that will make Polish language glottodidactics an important area and perceived as future-oriented. Although currently all the ac-tivities described are carried out on a narrower scope, their scale is still incom-parable to the educational offer proposed before the outbreak of the conflict in Ukraine. This fact is reinforced by the growing number of people migrating to Poland due to the work of citizens of countries from various, increasingly distant parts of the world, and the rapidly increasing number of Belarusians fleeing from persecution to our country.

Creating a clear long-term migration policy, including legal and organiza-tional assumptions for integration language courses, is becoming not only the need of the hour, but a much-awaited concept determining not only the future of further development and functioning of the state, but also of increasingly pro-fessionally engaged teachers, lecturers and other people. operating in the edu-cation space in the context of migration. The expectations of the Polish language glottodidactics community also include regulation of the profession of teacher and lecturer of Polish as a second language, development of an official curric-ulum for integration language courses, and standards of education and devel-opment of teachers and lecturers of Polish as a non-native language.

Their lack is responsible, first of all, for the lack of changes in the Polish language programs and glottodidactic paths of bachelor's, master's and post-graduate studies, which involve shifting the focus of the classes offered from the context of teaching Polish as a foreign language abroad to a second language in the context of migration in the country. Although the growing needs in the domestic educational labor market have significantly increased interest in this type of studies, universities have included in their programs content directly relating to teaching Polish as a second language in Poland to a small extent. The classes offered are still traditionally dominated by issues related to Polish as a foreign language. It is difficult to find courses that strengthen the particularly expected integration and inclusive dimension of a teacher's work, as well as workshops that strengthen psychosocial competences in the perspective of working in an intercultural environment. Their introduction seems to be con-ditioned by clearly defined requirements formulated in the form of official standards for the education of teachers and lectors of Polish as a non-native language (cf. Gębal, Miodunka 2023).

Mentioning teachers of Polish as a second language who carry out their ac-tivities in institutionalized education, it is worth paying attention to the dra-matically changing educational situation in Polish schools after the outbreak of the conflict in Ukraine. The number of students with migration experience in Polish schools, estimated at approximately 100,000, was supplemented by 342,000 Ukrainian refugees and war refugees of school age currently residing in Poland.

Although approximately half of this number of young Ukrainians, for unclear reasons, do not currently take advantage of the educational offer of Polish schools, taking classes remotely in Ukrainian schools or not fulfilling compulsory schooling at all, we have never had such a large number of students with experience in Polish schools. migration for whom Polish is a non-native language. Since the educational authorities have not basically modified the existing legislative and educational solutions integrating foreign children immigrating to Poland into the school system, concepts and assumptions are still being implemented, originally developed for much smaller needs in terms of the number of admitted students with migration experience and their cultural and linguistic specificity, largely limited to one nationality.

Ukrainian children and youth were offered initial education in Polish schools as part of specially launched preparatory units for students with migration experience, where, in addition to learning Polish as a second language, carried out for a short period of time (4–6 a week), subject classes are conducted in accordance with the requirements core curriculum of general education. A significant number of children and young people, especially in schools where their number was relatively small, were deprived of the opportunity to study in preparatory classes. In such situations, the educational obligation was carried out from the beginning of schooling in regular classes with children for whom Polish was their native language. It was complemented by additional classes in Polish as a second language for 4 hours.

The experiences of schools and individual teachers support the need to modify the organization of learning in preparatory classes, which, in the opinion of the teaching community, should, following the example of other European school systems, be limited only to intensive learning of the Polish language, reinforced with classes in the specialized language of school education and content supporting the development of competences. intercultural learners.

The list of issues for rapid systemic implementation in the institutionalized school context is quite long. It includes, among others: introducing a modified concept of preparatory classes with the subject Polish as a second language into the core curriculum of general education, regulating the profession of a teacher of Polish as a second language, developing standards for educating teachers of Polish as a non-native language, developing interculturally oriented textbooks for learning the language in the context of migration for individual educational stages, creating standards for linguistic, cultural and educational diagnosis for students admitted to Polish schools and introducing the teaching of Ukrainian as a foreign and inherited (origin) language in schools along with the possibility of passing eighth-grade and high school leaving exams in Ukrainian as a foreign language. Another issue requiring systemic regulation is the employment of Ukrainian teachers in Polish schools and the regulation of teaching and supporting activities of intercultural assistants increasingly engaged in Polish schools (cf. Gębal, Kumięga, Dembińska 2023).

The above considerations complement the experiences collected in the texts included in the entire volume. Their analysis argues for the need to modify the concepts of Polish language education currently developed and presented as part of studies for future teachers of Polish as a non-native language.

The teaching programs dedicated to students learning Polish as a foreign language, developed since the early 1990s, require the introduction of a number of changes due to the changing profile of the needs and expectations of modern learners. There is a strong need to develop curricula for teaching Polish as a second language, supported by catalogs that also describe the development of non-linguistic skills, supporting the ongoing acculturation processes and facilitating integration and inclusion activities. It is also worth preparing a curriculum addressed to the increasing number of learners who learn independently or in cooperation with others remotely, using the linguistic and educational potential of social media.

The need to develop program solutions for learning and teaching Polish as a second language also prompts reflection on the rapid need to develop new program solutions in the field of the language of professional communication and selected specialist languages, also in the varieties of the language of school education (cf. Schöne, Gębal, Kołsut 2015, Pamuła-Behrens, Szymańska 2018). The prepared programs and teaching materials should take into account the linguistic and cultural specificity of learners and the diversity of their previous educational experiences, for example by proposing solutions that are more related to the concept of intercultural teaching and multilingualism teaching, especially in relation to the Eastern Slavs, by proposing elements of inter-comprehensive teaching. It is also necessary to take into account the fact that more and more often those teaching Polish as a non-native language may be foreigners for whom Polish is not their native language. It is therefore suggested to develop appropriately prepared methodological guides for individual series of textbooks, which will facilitate preparation for classes in terms of language, teaching and methodology for this group of teachers.

The new educational reality calls for deeper reflection on the sense of creating the foundations of more personalized and differentiating concepts of teaching Polish as a non-native language, to a wider extent considering and respecting different learning styles and the educational autonomy of individual developing learning communities, created using the Internet and social networking sites.

Within the framework of the didactics outlined in this way, we can assume support for the further development of the didactic concepts and approaches mentioned at the beginning of our text, but in a slightly expanded form, considering new learning styles and ways of establishing communication contacts and undertaking linguistic activities.

In relation to the concept of action didactics, it is worth conducting a number of studies in the field of real communication and action needs within individual professional groups, and then based on them, developing multimodal packages of teaching materials, offering sets of case studies, global simulations, tasks and projects considering specific tasks in work environment, in a format for group classes and for self-taught students.

Intercultural didactics can use the concept of transcultural teaching to a wider extent, especially to a greater extent include Poland's regional diversity, in order to fit into the increasingly frequent migration movements of foreigners within Poland for private, family and professional reasons. It is also worth introducing a European perspective to a greater extent, thus preparing students for life and professional functioning in the European Community countries, to which some foreigners learning Polish will one day go.

With reference to the assumptions of multilingualism didactics and the above-mentioned intercomprehensive teaching, it is worth paying attention to the greater openness to making mistakes among Eastern Slavs teaching Polish, to the specific breakthrough of the culturally conditioned strong orientation towards the correctness of expression among East Slavic learners, also at beginner levels, which is largely required introducing intercompression techniques into the teaching process (cf. Gębal 2019, Izdebska-Długosz 2021, Saturno and Gębal 2022). To treat intercomprehension as a work technique that accelerates the language development of learners, and not mainly as an external factor strengthening fossilization (cf. Saturno and Gębal 2022).

From the perspective of the autonomy and reflexivity of the language education process, it is worth emphasizing the importance of learners' awareness of their own language development and pointing out its connections with thoughtful planning of further professional life in Poland. A look from this perspective should encourage the inclusion of elements of personalized education in the context of classes in the form of techniques and tools used during individual and group coaching and tutoring sessions.

Didactically, autonomy can be best expressed in strictly personalized classroom activities. Thanks to them, learners gain optimal conditions for the development of personal competences, including personal linguistic competence (Wilczyńska 2008) and personal competence in learning, both in the individual and social dimensions.

Bibliography

Dakowska M., 2010, *W poszukiwaniu wiedzy praktycznie użytecznej. O dojrzewaniu glottodydaktyki jako nauki,* "Neofilolog", 34, 9–20.

Długosz P., Kryvachuk L., Izdebska-Długosz D., 2022, *Uchodźcy wojenni z Ukrainy – życie w Polsce i plany na przyszłość,* Lublin: Wydawnictwo Academicon.

Europejski system opisu kształcenia językowego: uczenie się, nauczanie, ocenianie, 2003, Warszawa: Centralny Ośrodek Doskonalenia Nauczycieli.

Gębal P.E., 2010, *Dydaktyka kultury polskiej w kształceniu językowym cudzoziemców. Podejście porównawcze,* Kraków: Universitas.

Gębal P.E, 2019, *Dydaktyka języków obcych. Wprowadzenie,* Warszawa: Wydawnictwo Naukowe PWN.

Gębal P.E., Miodunka W.T., 2020, *Dydaktyka i metodyka nauczania języka polskiego jako obcego i drugiego,* Warszawa: Wydawnictwo Naukowe PWN.

Gębal P.E., Miodunka W.T., 2023, *Didactics of Polish as Foreign and Second Language against the European Background,* Göttingen: Vandenhoeck & Ruprecht Verlage (V&R unipress).

Gębal P.E., Kumięga Ł., Dembińska K., 2023, *Potrzeba regulacji zawodu nauczyciela/ lektora języka polskiego jako obcego/drugiego w perspektywie współczesnych wyzwań społecznych związanych z migracjami. Ekspertyza przygotowana na zlecenie Senatu RP,* https://www.senat.gov.pl/gfx/senat/userfiles/_public/k10/dokumenty/bad/2023/oe-46 2.pdf [04.03.2024].

Grucza F., 1978, *Glottodydaktyka, jej zakres i problemy,* "Przegląd Glottodydaktyczny", 1, 7–12.

Izdebska-Długosz D., 2021, *Błędy gramatyczne w polszczyźnie studentów ukraińskojęzycznych,* Kraków: Księgarnia Akademicka.

Miodunka W.T., 2016, *Glottodydaktyka polonistyczna. Pochodzenie – stan obecny – perspektywy,* Kraków: Księgarnia Akademicka.

Nawracka M., 2020, *Nauczanie języka polskiego jako obcego w perspektywie refleksyjnej i kulturowej,* Kraków: Księgarnia Akademicka.

Pamuła-Behrens M., Szymańska M., 2018, *Metodyka nauczania języka edukacji szkolnej uczniów z doświadczeniem migracji, Metoda JES-PL,* Warszawa: Ministerstwo Edukacji Narodowej.

Pfeiffer W., 2001, *Nauka języków obcych. Od praktyki do praktyki,* Poznań: Wagros.

Schöne K., Gębal P.E., Kołsut S., 2015, *Berufsspezifische Sprachkompetenzprofile,* Dresden: Technische Universität.

Saturno J., Gębal P.E., 2022, *Interkomprehensja w nauczaniu języka polskiego jako obcego (JPJO) Słowian wschodnich,* "Kształcenie Polonistyczne Cudzoziemców" Nr 29/2022, 213–229.

Wilczyńska W., 2008, *Autonomia a rozwijanie osobistej kompetencji komunikacyjnej,* "Języki Obce w Szkole" Nr 6/2008, 5–14.

Woźniewicz W., 1987, *Kierowanie procesem glottodydaktycznym,* Warszawa: Wydawnictwo Naukowe PWN.